TRANSMISSIONS
OF
EARTH
SPIRIT
WISDOM

A Shamanic Way of Seeing,
Being and Healing

"I must say that the incredible diversity and dimensionality of the wisdom and actual experiences of Amalia's new book is breathtaking in its scope and true vision. There's so much Life and Light within these pages and also real hope for a new and brighter scenario for Humankind. I place great value for all of us within these pages!"
—STEAVEN BROWN, SEDONA, AZ

"Amalia is mapping out what could seem a complex system with concise terminology. The reader can stay anchored in the proper understanding she is conveying about our consciousness, subconsciousness, and the journey to becoming aware of our unawareness and what we can do to overcome these hidden obstacles. Very well done in comparing these monumental aspects of humanity, which allows the reader to come to their own conclusions of where they stand."
—ED BENOIT, SEDONA, AZ

"What a wondrous journey Amalia has taken me on. It was a deep lesson in awareness through her so very interesting and contemplative inner and outer world. She showed me how to see both my world and the world through a sacred lens of intent, purity of heart and deep reverence and gratitude for life."
—DOTTY O DONNELL, BOSTON, MA

"Amalia unabashedly draws a series of pertinent, and potentially life-transforming, realizations from her own inner wellspring. She affirms that the beauty of the Sacred Mystery itself is capable of spurring each of us onward to new heights of more refined realization!"
—LOREN LEWISOHN, HAWAII

"A wonderful style of weaving personal stories into teachings, which highly captures the attention of the reader."
—BARBARA BRYAN, SEDONA, AZ

TRANSMISSIONS
OF
EARTH
SPIRIT
WISDOM

A Shamanic Way of Seeing,
Being and Healing

AMALIA CAMATEROS

The Awakened Press

For information about special discounts or for bulk purchases,
please contact The Awakened Press at books@theawakenedpress.com.

The Awakened Press can bring authors to your live event.
For more information or to book an event contact
books@theawakenedpress.com or
visit our website at www.theawakenedpress.com.

Cover and book design, David Moratto
Book editor, Lindsay R.A. Dierking
Earth Spirit Wisdom logo designed by Amalia Camateros

Printed in the United States of America
First The Awakened Press trade paperback edition

ISBN: 979-8-9881800-8-1

*The more we connect with Mother Nature,
the more she helps us understand and know ourselves.*

To all who yearn, desire, and aspire to bring more conscious awareness to body, self, others, our planet and beyond.

The body of work herein is not so much granted from what I am personally invested to share, but what the bank of my soul wishes to impart to the greater world. As a legacy of what has been gleaned and garnered over my life's work in service as a naturopathic doctor, psycho-spiritual and shamanic healer, empowerment guide and ceremonial priestess, it is for you I dedicate this book.

I bestow and entrust this imparted wisdom for the guidance of aligning you to your True and Authentic Self and in assisting to balance your emotional body, quieting your mind, and inspiring your spirit to extend and expand beyond the limitations of the mechanical mind.

To our beloved planet, Mother Earth, and all that you provide to sustain us and the sanctuary of living sanctity and wisdom you eternally offer. Thank you, thank you, thank you.

Contents

WISDOM

The Way of the Book

It is with much delight that I now share this bank of wisdom that I have gleaned through the trials and tribulations, along with the high peaks of revelation of my life's journey with you.

The main body of this book was laid down many years ago at a writer's retreat with Tom Bird, writer instructor and publisher. We were to write our book in the automatic stream of inspiration, following and trusting the "inner writer," without even as much as a doubt or second thought to what flowed through.

Flashes of brilliance also wove their way into my shamanic healing sessions with my clients with astounding metaphors. As they arose, my attention was struck with immediacy and urgency to take note to share them with you at some time. That time is now.

The wisdom in this book has trickled up from the artesian waters of the ground, from the deep roots of living trees, from the agents of power: the elements of earth, water, fire and air, from the rock spirits and the thunder beings. It has come through the bolts of brilliance that awoke me from my deepest sleep and the breakthrough realizations that surfaced during my meditations. Much of the insights, and directives too, gleamed through like gold as I shone the light of awareness in the darkest, most hidden parts of my shadow self.

The excerpts herein have been scribed and transmitted from the highest, genuine and candid place in me that I have come to know.

They have been collated into a compendium that will ignite your awareness, touch in on your deeper sense of knowing, help you navigate your wayward emotions and encourage a firm posture of balance.

In their simplicity and boldness, these insights usher you through a sine wave of deep-rooted wisdom that take you into the depths of contemplation and also raise you to the heights of viewing. In this compendium, the high and lighter side of the wave comes through with corresponding allegory and metaphor that are utilized to keep the balance of levity, while the current of wisdom runs deep and wide. For example, the excerpt "Chasing the Dragon's Tail" stands for the metaphor of the ability to tame your inner dragon and the wild thoughts of your unruly mind. The deepest level of truth, more often than not, has a built-in heightened sense of humor that can make the experience more palatable and digestible.

Learning through allegory and metaphor can more readily bypass the intellectual brain and can land in the extra-sensory and subconscious mind. This instills the kernel of knowledge to be not only planted but also grounded into the wisdom body of self. The synergy of truth, experience, and heartfelt intention coalesce into the prose of a language that settles in your body with a sense of balanced equanimity and composure. Assimilation and absorption can thus be made through both the thought and feeling realms.

The insights in this book are not new, for truth is truth. They are presented in such a way as to stretch the edges of your awareness and expand the limitations of perception that may be asking for a heightened vantage point of understanding. All in all, offering a simple, yet profound way of looking at life and its teachings.

You may be triggered throughout somewhat as these writings are not for the fainthearted. Like Zen Sticks, they can strike your attention from the slump of complacency to awaken your clarity, vision and mindfulness. Shamanic in essence, they can shed light on your hidden shadow self, and ask it to step into the forefront to be seen and accepted. They can summon you to go beyond what the limited eye can see, to perceive through the eyes of your own inner shaman.

These writings can bridge the gap between the material world and conscious mind and the Spirit World of your inner self.

The path of evolution urges us to grow beyond the limitations we have been stuck in and to take the journey that asks us to expand beyond our comfort zones. Herein is your invitation to stretch and expand beyond the mechanized mind.

Throughout these excerpts I have capitalized some words to emphasize their prominence to bring distinction to their meaning and purpose. An example is the word "Spirit" when it is used in the sense of a consciousness of the Universe, compared with the "spirit" of such a thing. Matter, Masculine and Feminine, Sun and Moon, God-Given and The All That Is have also been given regard in this manner.

I have also taken the liberty of using words that have pushed their way into my conscious awareness through dream and meditation and a slip of the tongue that I call "Fusion Words." These are two words that stream together to create a common denominator to create an idiom or new expression, such as *realationship* (a real relationship), or *potentiallity* (a potential of all your totality), which bring more to the plate in the world of prose and phrase.

To bring a flow of ease for the reader, the excerpts are arranged in three sections of Earth, Spirit and Wisdom.

From a grounded standpoint, the excerpts within the body of this work are not offered merely as disembodied words but as grounded capsules of wisdom. They are a shamanic type of medicine to give you a deeper perspective into the nature of self and planetary healing.

Every passage has been received as a small, bite-sized discourse that stands on its own merits and therefore reads as a singular download, each complete in its own right. Whether you read them one at a time, or back-to-back, allow yourself time to chew (contemplate), digest (absorb) and assimilate (integrate) into your life what truly resonates for you.

Each excerpt will stretch the edges of your perspective and trigger the idle points of consciousness to instigate and inspire your awakening. They will steer you back into your own lane, ground your energy into your true alignment, and assist you in staying focused, balanced, centered and connected to the greater whole.

I am presenting these insights as transmitted through my direct experience and invite you to contemplate the messages and meanings offered with an openness to decipher what resonates with you. Let it steep into the cauldron of self and let go of the rest.

They will instigate your own viewpoints and visions that you may wish to write down to let them land all the way into the ground of your being.

Ultimately, it is for you to make your own conscious decisions that are drawn from your own experiences and insights, as they will always lead you to the most authentic version of your self-truth.

May you garner from this book what serves you for your highest good and walk your Earth Walk in the sanctity of your truest and authentic self.

—AMALIA CAMATEROS
*I would love to hear from you, please feel free to
share your responses to amalia@earthspiritwisdom.com.*

THE ALL THAT IS

Seek not that which you do not already have within yourself, for there is nothing in the world that can be given to you that you do not already have within the deeper space of your inner being. Our mind and spirit-force are not separate from our souls, and our souls are not separate from All That Is. We are each vital ingredients in the creation of this cosmic soup, and even though it may not feel like it, we are at all times connected to Creation.

Open up; *open* to all that you are and can be, draw from the "within place" of your own being, from the totality of Self. Each of us have access to this all-ness of Creation when we stop and sit quietly and reverently with this most truest of Self.

In the field and meadows of time, flowers, plants and trees proclaim their interconnection to the All That Is, showing us, "This is how to be in your own perfect essence. Grow up out of the dark soil of your life and grow sturdy and strong into the highest reaches of light. Let your petals unfurl and bloom into the grace and embrace of God's silent knowing, where all becomes realized and true."

Do not bind yourself up in the knots of can-nots... "I can't do it; I am not enough; it is available for others but not for me..." This keeps you in the illusion that you are separate from the garden of creation and imprisons you in your own self-mind-made machinations that you are indeed unworthy of blooming into the fullness of Self.

We are all seemingly separate and yet connected to the whole. Like the flower in the field of plenty, you too are one among us all that is bountiful, beauteous, pure, loving and divine. The soil, the air and the water, like the body, mind and spirit, are intrinsically connected in their entirety. The clouds are not separate from the sky, the sun is not separate from the light, the waves are not separate from the ocean, our feet are not separate from our legs and our legs are not separate from our bodies. We need all the seemingly separate parts to make the beautiful world of self and beyond whole, and to realize we are already complete as we continue to grow in the garden of life.

ACTIVATION

When you are out in nature, take a moment to observe a tree in its entirety. Be aware of its unseen roots, its trunk, its branches and leaves, and acknowledge the many parts that make up its absoluteness, its wholeness. Then expand your vision to become aware of surrounding trees, then extend your perspective to embrace the extended family of trees on the planet. Each appears to be separate, and yet is one and the same.

EARTH

Beginning with Earth, this section holds the ground for what the elements of nature and the shamanic realm are revealing to us. It invites us to bear witness to, connect with and embody the teachings of Mother Earth as a greater part of our selves.

What the Bleep Is This?

Look at the wonder and marvel of this, our planet, Mother Earth. She is an intricate lattice of life, interwoven into a tapestry of one living, breathing organism.

Notice the benevolence of love as she extends her caring arms to embrace all life. Look around at the majesty of hers and all of Creation—the trees, the sky, the stars, the flowers, our hearts—beating with the rhythm of life itself.

The trillions of cellular organisms in our bodies work in unison for the benefit of the whole. One has to ask, "Who or what has created this magnificent perfection?" The separate pieces are put in place so exactly and distinctly to create a mosaic masterpiece.

Why are we so nonchalant and dispassionate about life in all of its magnificence? Why do we live our existence from day to day as we turn a blind eye to this magic that awaits us in every moment? This magic gives birth from seed to fruit, from ova to human, and from thought to matter, from no-thing to everything.

Tune into and use your extra-sensory vision to see through the veils of complacency. Be the watcher, the seer, the sage, the shaman, and take a step back to witness the greater design of perfection taking place.

Take a deep breath to inhale this magnificence. Let this perfection move in and through your body, for this is where you absorb the sustenance of all of life: in the body.

Who are our creators, our designers, and our prime movers?

Could it be an intelligence from another galaxy or from another time-place continuum? Or could it be our divine Mother/Father God, of whom we get too busy to remember; that which lies deeply within the imaginal cells of our beings—the original seed-cell of our entirety?

How have we become so complacent with this super-natural wonderment we call life on planet Earth?

We have become fragmented with the list of things to do that keeps us busy beyond reparation. We fray our energy and allow it to dangle from an outer limb in space. We must return our attention and sight inward and into the one cell within that knows its origin of place—the one point of light that streams the light of Mother/Father God within and through us.

The One who has been traversing with us throughout time—the inner voice and knowing has been with us all along. That same inner grounded, seemingly stern yet loving voice that has spoken to us throughout our lifetime (and perhaps lifetimes) has not changed, has not altered or faltered, but brings with it the love, guidance and benevolence for our greatest good.

Could it be the one resounding voice of God, of the All That Is that has the same way of speaking to us all? Does it speak to every cell in each of our bodies? How does it entrain our cells to act in unison as one living organism?

Let us not forget how amazing we truly are: a miracle of God's creation. Let us use our vision-sense to truly see this most perfect of designs.

ACTIVATION

We must continue to ask questions to keep our minds and hearts open to the magic that Mother Earth and all of Creation provides. Questions such as: "What the bleep is this?" "How can I live in full respect and wonder of this creation?" "What more can I do to add to the beauty of this life?"

Stone Seers and Sages

Let us take a look at the large rocks and stones of our planet. They are planted and rooted in their solidity and stillness. They don't run or hide from oncoming challenges, they don't cower from the scorching sun, complain about the icy snow or recoil from the strong wind gales. Nor are they afraid of the black night sky or get offended when passing birds defacate on them! They show us instead to ground our energy and how to be strong and firm in our stance. As silent seers, they watch and witness all that passes by without retorting or reacting. Survivors of time, they have withstood cataclysms throughout the ages and still remain intact to this day.

Rocks are solid and stable like our backbones that hold us upright with strength, keeping the rest of our body in place. The Diné (Navajo People) of the Southwestern United States of America regard rocks as the bones of the Earth, holding the structure of our Earth in place. Rocks not only reflect the moral fiber of Earth's spiritual standing, but also contain a potent storehouse of geological information. This is similar to our own bodies, where the bone structure keeps the rest of our bodies in place and stores our genetic information.

Like sentient sages and the humble gurus of our time, rocks and stones teach us to be present, right here and right now, with emptiness of thought. They remind us to "be" in the presence of existence.

They are anchors of universal energy that are grounded in their being, with nowhere to go and nowhere to run. Through their very mode of being, they become catalysts for our own evolution. If you let them, they can teach you how to drop into your being in a calm, centered, and grounded way.

Have we become too busy to connect with these wisdom teachers that Mother Earth presents to us? Are we too restless and impatient to get present enough to receive all that is intended for us of Earth's bounty? Our human race is rushing to get things done, running on an endless treadmill to "get ahead" into the so-called future of our making. We have lost the grounded and stable nature that these rock beings remind us of. We have become disconnected from the ground of our being, from the magic that the simplicity of nature affords us.

Let us learn from these stone seers, where the rock masters stand still and firm, and take heed to what these teachers have to say. We may just learn something that could change and improve the course of our lives.

The spirit of the stones is available to us at all times. We merely need to stop and listen into their silence, into the stillness that they themselves embody and exhibit. *When you are silent the stones speak.* They are living libraries of Earth-space continuum that anchor the Spirit of place and are living portals to the Wisdom of the Earth and of the Universe that is available to each and every one of us.

ACTIVATION

The next time you find yourself in the company of some large rocks, sit with your backbone against the face of the rock. Allow yourself to sink down into the depth of Earth's energy and with your deeper sense of being. Emulate the rock to let it show you how to sit in stillness, in emptiness of thought, grounded to the earth like itself. In this place with nowhere to go or nothing to do, just be present, be with the silence within and acknowledge the rocks' and your own ancient beingness.

Get Grounded:
Out of Our Heads, into
Our Bodies and into the Earth

We spend so much time in our heads, letting our thoughts direct our way. The mind continuously splits our focus with an "and," an "or" or a "but." Like a ping-pong match, our thoughts thrash back and forth. Nowadays, our thoughts have become so much more hyperactive that our minds are more like a pinball machine ricocheting from one thought to another in all angles and directions, leading us astray, further from the truth of our hearts as we move along our path.

We consequently get jammed in our thoughts and stuck in our heads, eliciting the feeling of "going crazy." The effect of this is that it creates an intensified, static noise, creating a field of incoherence, making it almost impossible to maintain clarity of thought. Instead of being monopolized by this repetitive sequence, we can utilize and harness this electrical field to our advantage and employ its energy for our overall benefit. By directing this excess energy IN and DOWN through our bodies, from the top of the head where the electrical charge is generated, and channeling it down into the base of our spines and then into the Earth, we can ground this energy. This helps us get out of our heads, into our bodies and into the Earth!

Mother Earth is a power point from which we can plug ourselves into at all times. This not only releases what we no longer need, but draws up the endless supply of her bountiful energy as fuel for our bodies. At the same time, here is where we can connect with something far steadier than our own minds and secure ourselves with her stable energy.

The trees teach us how to do this in the simplest of ways. They plunge their roots deep into Earth, teaching us to drop our energy and connect with the ground beneath our feet so that we can stand tall in our trunks, and raise our branches high to receive the full light of day. They teach us to stand our ground, claim our stance, be strong and sturdy on our feet, and hold our heads high with our arms extended lovingly to share the fruit of our being.

Trees also teach us about the balance of the Yin and Yang (strength and flexibility), the Above and Below (connecting Earth to Sky), the Seen and the Unseen (the roots below the earth and the trunk and branches above), the Light and the Dark (how it channels the light of day, taking the sun's energy all the way down into the dark soil), all of which become integral parts of the whole. They stand in balance between both worlds.

The trees show us that if they don't put down their roots and take a stronghold on the Earth, a strong gale, flood or storm could uproot them, and they could die. If they don't sink their roots down deep to drink from the deeper well and draw up the minerals and sustenance from their roots, they may not survive the summer seasons. Just like trees, we need to plant ourselves firmly on the ground to stand tall and strong, to draw nourishment from Mother Earth, and tap into and connect with something greater than our smaller and stunted self.

If we are grounded, stable and secure like trees, we are less likely to be taken off guard, off balance and become uprooted in our lives. Being grounded helps us withstand the oncoming weather and storms in our lives, the challenging moments in our relationships, the struggles with our finances and our governments, the loss of confidence and our own mind-made machinations that can topple us over.

A tree cannot exist without its roots no more than we can exist and evolve without our own roots of our ancestors and of our connection with Mother Earth. Earth is the most undying ancestor we are heirs to. We have roots, too! Not through the chain of our family tree of our ancestry alone, but through our very own nervous systems, right in our own bodies, in our legs that plant themselves on the Earth every day of our lives through our sciatic nerves. Our sciatic nerves are the largest nerves in the body and actually look like tree roots! They flow the current of nerve energy from the base of our spine down to our legs and feet in order to run from danger and move us forward. They serve as the two prongs of an electrical cord that can plug into the socket or power point of Mother Earth to activate our higher power and potential.

Just like a blender on the kitchen counter that needs to be plugged into the socket in order to activate what it is designed to do, we too are like an appliance that needs to be connected to the greater power source of Mother Earth. As we plant our roots into the greater grid, we connect to the electromagnetic current that activates more of our life potential. A blender is still a blender and we are still human but not until we are switched on can we fulfill what we have come here to do.

We could say that we are human trees, so the more we connect into the energy of this source, the more we can stand on our own two feet, the more we can stretch our branches out into the greater world, and the more fruit we can bear and share with others.

How to ground your energy with Mother Earth:

This exercise is best practiced with bare feet on the ground but can also be effective wherever you may be. Even in a high-rise building you can still ground your energy!

Stand with feet parallel and shoulder-width apart (barefoot is most beneficial when standing on the earth wherever possible). This is to allow the connection of your root chakra, the energy center at the base of the spine at the perineum between the anus and the genitals, to have a clear thoroughfare to Earth. Take a moment to visualize what your inner tree looks like. Is it strong or weak? Is it broad, or thin and tall? Are its roots deep or are they shallow? Ask your inner tree what it needs. More water? To deepen the roots? More tending? More love? More sunlight? Be authentic in your answers, for they will provide guidance as to your next step on your way to your health and can mirror your emotional self and what you need in order to get stronger in yourself.

Now take a few deep, long breaths in through the nose and exhale through the mouth to let go and surrender. Release the steam to let go some of the pressure.

With a deep inhale, followed by a long and slow exhale, follow your awareness of the breath all the way down from the head to the root chakra. Allow your awareness to settle there for a moment before you follow your sciatic nerves down the thighs, down the knees, the shins, the ankles, and all the way down and into your feet. Breathe in through the nose and out of the mouth...and continue doing so throughout.

Once you get to the feet, visualize streaming your inner roots down into the Earth and keep following them down... Further down through the soil, the roots of other trees, the rocks, through the deeper interior layers of inner Earth, and even down deeper. Follow your roots until you sense Earth's core, where Mother Earth's heart is.

Once you sense the core of Earth Mother, what color do you see or sense? What shape is it? What does it look like? Is it made from liquid fire? Dark soil? Molten lava? A bright, brilliant sun? Is it moving? How fast or how slow? What energy does it carry? What emotion does she portray? Passion? Unconditional Love? Wrath? Peace? Power?

Now listen in to her, connect your roots with her... Go right there into the color, the sound, the feeling, and tap into and connect your roots with her and listen to the deeper wisdom of Mother Earth...

What advice does she give you at this time? Trust it and know it, for it is not separate from yourself as this energy you see and feel is yours. It is a living mirror of your own intrinsic energy. For she is the greater part of your own living being and the greater body of humanity.

Thank Mother Earth, with an inner bow to her in honor of all that she is and does and then draw up this essential wisdom, this nourishment from your taproots. Begin from her core and see her energy running up your roots. Drink up her energy, the color, the feeling she supplied you with. Let it run up your roots and nourish your body like she does for the trees.

Bring this energy up through the feet, up the knees, the thighs and all the way up through the body, into the bones, the flesh, the cells and the spaces between the cells, the blood, refueling your body with her Shakti, her Life Force Energy. See this energy stream and fill every part of your body: the organs, neck, spine, face, eyes, ears, brain, and all the way up through the crown chakra at the top of your head. Your entire body is infused with whatever you felt and witnessed at the core of Earth, her heart.

Now allow the stream of this energy to flow out of the top of your head like a fountain, flowing all around you like a continuous stream, 360 degrees around you. This will clear, strengthen and nourish your inner tree and clean your aura and luminous light field. As it streams down to the Earth, let it merge with the current from under your feet and breathe it back up into your heart, up through your crown again and around your body.

Repeat this entire process once more to let the energy stream through like a miraculous fountain that can replenish and restore your sense of being. As you bring Mother Earth's energy up once again to the top of the head, raise your arms simultaneously like large branches of a glorious tree and stretch up to the light. Then as you breathe out, lower the arms slowly and usher the light all around your body again. See the color you saw at Earth's core surrounding and protecting you and finish with hands in prayer position in front of your heart.

Remember to loosen and shake off the old, dead leaves from your branches and let them fall with a long, slow exhale into the earth on the downswing of your arms. Let the heavy feelings and the entanglements of the mind drop into the Earth to be recycled for renewable energy. This way we can be more present not only in our own lives, but with life as a whole.

Mother Earth knows exactly what to do with dead leaves, dead bodies, the tears, the blood, and the pain. She is alive and well and knows how to recycle, transmute and utilize what you no longer need as fertilizer to enliven your body-being.

Mother Earth wastes nothing and knows what to do and how to do it. She has been doing it a lot longer than we have been around and as a master of alchemy, she transmutes death into life, stress into ease, confusion into simplicity.

Earth is the founder ancestor. We were born on her and from her. She is a living library, the keeper of our genetic codes. Like a friend of mine, Mirakle W.L. King, once said… "HOME stands for Here On Mother Earth." She is the planet we call *home*; this is our home. We are not here to stand on her, but *with* her, accepting and loving her as the greater part of our own being.

ACTIVATION

The next time you are confronted with feelings you would much rather release, let go and shake out your crammed thoughts like dead leaves to the ground by practicing this exercise I have called, "The Inner Tree of Light." I made my own video of this practice and its simple teachings on my website: earthspiritwisdom.com on my videos page, which will give you a clearer understanding of this process.

Standing Trees

There are many cultures within the mythological, religious and philosophical traditions that venerate the Mother Tree as a symbol of the root of their existence. As a tree of life, a world tree or a cosmic tree, she is revered as a tree of knowledge that connects Heaven to the Underworld and to the adherence of all life.

Standing at the center of Creation, her roots are tapped deep into the great unknown, into the Underworld, and her branches extend to the farthest reaches of the universe of the Overworld. She is the symbol of life-ever-giving.

As descendants and soul seeds of this tree, we land from Spirit to Matter, from Sky to Earth, planted into the ground of our being. Just like trees, our life cycle begins with conception (seed), to birth (sprout), to infancy (seedling), to juvenile (sapling), to adult (mature tree), to elderly (declining tree) and finally, to death (decomposition of the tree), which then feeds and nourishes the soil in preparation for the next generation. We are a part of an intricate flow of coming and going and an interconnected part of the elemental world that surrounds and sustains us.

Just like the Great Matriarch World Tree that stands as the central axis of our cosmos, planetary trees teach us how to live in accordance with the greater weave of this living matrix. They show us how to stand firm and securely by connecting our roots with our feet planted to the ground. They demonstrate how to stand strong in our trunks as we reach for the light of the heavens with our branches—our arms. They teach us to share our strengths and abundance with each other, just as the mother trees that are the biggest and oldest trees in the forest "suckle their young" by pumping liquid sugar into their youngs' roots when they are too weak and small to reach the light in deeply shaded areas. Or they draw up water with their deep roots to make it more available to shallow-rooted seedlings and send neighbor trees nutrients that struggle nearby. Trees are connected to each other through the deeper lattice of roots that are laid down as a matrix of fortification, creating a living support system for one another.

Throughout our modern history, however, there has been a general consensus that trees compete with each other to strive and survive as disconnected entities competing for sunlight, nutrients and water. Studies made by modern scientists and foresters such as Peter Wohlleben and Suzanne Simard authenticate that this is not so. In their research, they have found that trees are not resource-grabbing entities that compete against each other, but rather, they demonstrate how to live in an interlinking system that can work in harmony and in support of each other. Instead, trees thrive in cooperation for the greater welfare of their species by communing with the underground fungal networks (the "wood-wide-web") as they exchange sugar and carbon for water and nutrients. (Peter Wohlleben, *The Hidden Life of Trees* [Vancouver, BC, Canada: Greystone Books Ltd., 2015, 2016] and Suzanne Simard, "Suzanne Simard: Research," SuzanneSimard.com, Suzanne Simard, accessed December 5, 2023. https://suzannesimard.com/research/.)

We are also woven into an intricate and vital symbiotic relationship with trees. For trees breathe in what we breathe out (carbon dioxide—our toxic waste) and we breathe in what they breathe out (pure oxygen—a life-giving property). They are the greater living lungs of the human world and of the Earth itself. We need them as much as they need us. Human civilization could well assimilate and acculturate how the trees have managed to preserve and conserve their species for over 350 million years. They are a simple, symbiotic template that we can adopt in order to remember the deeper connection we share with each other in sharing our resources for the betterment of the greater whole.

No, we are not alone in the plight of survival. Trees remind us how to support and promote one another's growth and progress in the human-wide-web. While at the center of Creation, the Great Mother Tree upholds the living template to flourish within our greater thrival.

ACTIVATION

Plant your feet on the ground or floor on which you stand and acknowledge the lattice of tree roots under your feet that remind you that you can be nourished by the Earth. Become cognizant of the symbiotic relationship that we have with trees so that when you breathe out, they breathe in and when we breathe in, they breathe out. Stand at the center of your universe—your creation—like the Great Mother Tree, and feel the greatness that you stand on, in and for.

Weeding Our
Inner Gardens

The gardeners of the world would each tell you, "First, you need to pull out the weeds before you plant your flowers in a garden bed." They would also tell you that it is wise to prepare the soil by tilling it and adding a high nutrient, such as fertilizer, before you plant your seeds to ensure a healthy and abundant crop return.

Most things, I have found, take time in the preparation stage to create a good outcome. I first learned this rudimentary lesson when I was married in my earlier years and in the process of building our first home. When I was not seeing my naturopathic clients at work, I would help out where I could to finish our home together.

After my client work, I would come home to my husband working on the house diligently and ask him what I could do next.

"You can paint the door," he suggested. I then grabbed the paint and brush with vigor and excitement, opened the lid and stirred the paint, then dipped the paintbrush in the paint ready to slap the brush on the bare wood door.

He stopped me in my tracks right before the paint touched the wood. "What are you doing?" He was perplexed.

"I am painting the door," I innocently answered.

He proclaimed that when painting a door, you cannot just slap paint on a door that is not prepared correctly. "Amalia, you can't just grab a paintbrush and paint the door; it is not as simple as that. You need to first sand the door down, fill in the cracks with filler, then you have to sand the door down one more time and then you can start painting."

I was confounded and disappointed, and what started out as a keen inspiration ended in a burdensome task. I couldn't believe I had to go through all those steps in order to get to the good part!

I did sand the door, filled the cracks, sanded some more, and then when I painted the door it looked perfect, professional, and in good stead with the rest of our beautiful home.

I learned a very strong lesson that day: You cannot just gloss or paint over things and expect a smooth result... You need to go step by step along the way in order to produce a finished product.

Back in the garden... The same application is required. You need to pull the weeds out, till the soil, add nutrients to it, and let it sit before you plant your garden in order for it to thrive! Otherwise, the flowers and seedlings will be strangulated by ignorance and impatience.

Equivalently, we need to pull out the weeds that crowd our mind to release the incessant chatter, old and limiting thought patterns, programs, and past hurts that stifle our inner soil for change.

We need to exercise, dance, write, relax, and breathe out the worries and entanglements of our minds to make space for new and innovative ideas to spring forth from the soil of our consciousness. Thus allowing new and innovative ideas, alternative pathways and fresh approaches to situations that will increase the blooming of goodness in our lives and inner gardens.

ACTIVATION

Give yourself time to ascertain the necessary steps along the way to prepare your inner soil of consciousness. Take a step back and look at your inner garden bed. What needs clearing here? What are your next steps of action in order to produce a bountiful harvest?

By adopting this simple strategy, you can more fully enjoy the fruits of your bountiful garden.

We each desire to be fulfilled (to be fully filled). To accomplish this, we need an open space that is clear enough to fill with our new seeds of intent.

Blessed Bee in
the Greater Hive

I believe we can learn a lot from the bees in making a shift from survival to thrival, from crawling aimlessly, estranged and disconnected, to moving in a synthesis of union for the greater good of all.

Up until this point, for the most part, humanity continues its undertakings single-handedly, like ants who carry a huge load on their backs one by one, soldiering on, painstakingly. It seems to take an overriding crisis in our lives to join our efforts to work as one unit to give our helping hands to each other. The 911 bombing of the Twin Towers in New York City was a good demonstration of how catastrophes can jolt us out of our self-seeking and self-centered dispositions. It is through such promptings that we often pool our efforts together to clean up the debris, feed those who are hungry, clothe those who are cold, pray for those in need and behave as one hive as the bees have illustrated for millions of years.

For 130 million years, bees, one of the earliest known insects on our planet, have adapted and evolved into a highly intelligent and organized society. Up to 80,000 bees work together as one superorganism, one moving unit, each has their specific tasks and roles in the colony as either worker bees, guard bees, nurse bees, drone bees, cleaner bees, forager bees, undertaker bees, builder bees, temperature controllers and of course, the Queen Bee, who produces up to two thousand eggs per day. She is the matriarchy, the central figure of the matrix from which the hive revolves. Not only do bees cross-pollinate to fertilize our flora, but they also produce honey that supplies us with a myriad of nutrients rich in vitamins, proteins and minerals, along with the delight of its sweetness. The bee's venom has throughout history been used in apitherapy (bee sting therapy) for its powerful medicinal properties that range from reducing inflammation to treating chronic illnesses. Bees also provide us with a regional working template for a progressive future, all working together for the survival and thrival of the whole.

When honeybees build their comb, they work in teams and employ a festooning process whereby they literally span across a broad area by linking to each other's legs, establishing a long line to form a bridge. Trees also employ a similar process in communicating their needs by sending each other necessary nutrients via a network of latticed fungi deep in the soil. Their deep roots extend to each other, and in effect hold hands like bees to create a bridge of communication and support for each other's growth.

Mother Earth is our Queen Bee, our greater mother who serves and continually provides for us so that we are nourished in the greater hive. *"As we sit around the circle and suppose, the truth sits in the center and knows"*—this is a wonderful quote by an unknown author evoking the metaphor that humanity points the finger at everyone else in the circle, blaming and shaming, scamming and cramming, while the Earth Mother is in truth, at the center of the matrix generating consistently and quietly the thrum and thrive of the greater hive.

We could employ the template of how the bees work, diligently and selflessly, to create the perfect environment to ensure that Queen Bee (Mother Earth) has all she needs to do her job well, to ensure that future generations of the greater hive are secured. The fabric of our society is torn and frayed. We have scrambled and spun our wheels incessantly to "get ahead" or "do better than our neighbors" at each other's expense. We are not pooling our resources together and working as one unit.

Bees show us how to move as one organism, one mind, one intelligent society. We need not strive to get ahead, but to get on with it. This does not mean that we lose face of our unique abilities, for we can each show up with our specialty, our mastery (just like the bees do) to add to the value of each other's lives and the greater whole. We can show up for the Greater Good of All, to ensure that we enjoy the privilege of a life everlasting. The sweet taste of honey, the nectar of life, can be savored from one generation to the next.

Here is an excerpt on bees from my first book, *Spirit of The Stones,* from Chapter 7, "The Yucatán Transmissions":

> *Bees work for the royal one, the Queen. May bees build their hives as a temple for the Queen in which to preserve the heritage of the royal lineage and in guardianship of the inherent knowledge. Bees work incessantly for the Silent One at the center, who has the instinct to keep the state of affairs balanced and amenable to the Gods. The hive is a template of the Mayan Kingdoms, where many busy workers constructed temples of worship for their royal kings and queens, high priests, priestesses, and lords. These were places from which the highest, clearest communications from the Gods were heard and then put into service for the people and their lands. The work of the bees here continues, anchoring the game plan, the regional working template for a progressive future.*

ACTIVATION

How can you employ the festooning process of holding hands with others to create a bridge of success for all involved? In which way can you serve the greater good? What unique quality do you hold at the center of your inner self that could be shared with the greater hive?

Symphony of
Reciprocation

It was during my visit to Australia, visiting my family, when on a bright and sunny day I took an investigative walk around the suburban neighborhood in which they live. They happen to live right beside a ten-lane freeway, which is not something I am used to in regard to the noise, pollution, and ghastly sight of rows of cars edging and dodging around each other to save a few more moments in the day. What I am accustomed to is the silence of the megalithic red rocks, the caw of the ravens, the open expanse of terrain and the spiny desert cacti of Sedona, Arizona, U.S.A.

I knew there was a large parkland in the close vicinity and set out to find it to restore my sanctity. It took me at least forty minutes to scout the area, using only my inner compass to arrive at the nature park. After the constant drone of the traffic, I was searching for a deeper peace, where I could drop into and deeply relax after bracing myself in the suburbs of Melbourne.

When I arrived in the green and lush nature-land, I took a long, deep breath. I was surrounded by eucalyptus gum trees, inexhaustible bird life and insects all abounding in the simplest of ways—only minutes away from the ten-lane freeway, all of life was simple and free. There, as the centerpiece, lay a shapely, curvaceous lake, placid and serene was its temperament of the day.

I found my own private spot and sat in agreeable witness to the beauty with a naked eye and earnest ear. I became cognizant of what is going on at all times, regardless of whether we are there or not. The wind moved across the water, creating ripples along the surface of the lake, the reeds swayed to and fro in the gentle breeze, the rustle of the eucalyptus trees hushed the noise of the nearby traffic, the ducks swept across the water's edge and the sun cast jewels of light on the water's surface like diamonds glistening in a pitch-black sky. The visual composition of aesthetic beauty and surround-sound of each element composed a perfect, grand symphony of orchestral splendor.

Life in bustling cities and suburbia exhibit the colliding elements of segregated and separate components to form the whole. Machinery, signs, traffic, rules and regulations create a field of discordance, propagating pressure, stress and tension. These are not environments conducive to opening the senses, or for taking a deeper inhale to "let it all in" or to see the greater picture. The sharp staccato sounds of such environments also lend themselves to creating a more separated and segregated framework, at the expense of seeing and experiencing the greater whole. As the nervous system adjusts to our external stimuli, it braces itself against the abrasion of discordance to protect itself. In response, our bodies produce stress hormones such as cortisol and adrenaline to deal with the stress, which further promotes the onset of insidious stress.

Even though the city has its high points in the arts and culture, and is teeming with creativity, Mother Nature, in her organic and generative creation, embraces all that she provides. Insects, plants, animals, rocks, trees and all elements have their perfect place in the harmony of her divine symphony. Each element seems to act on behalf of and in response with each other in higher consonance. Each act is a note of music, all working in perfect pitch and unison to create a greater harmonic. Each reciprocates their appreciation with the exaltation of praise to the greater mother, Mother Earth, for the gift of all life.

It is within Mother Nature where we can take that deeper breath and drop into the organic nature of self within the workings of the greater whole. It is here where we can take a moment to clear the mind and truly listen, with full appreciation of the magic of living moments that life can bring. It is in this appreciation of such beauty that we, too, can reciprocate our gratitude for all of life.

ACTIVATION

Seek out your parks, your lakes and your nature zones to attune to the beauty of Mother Nature. Observe the simple action of natural beauty; listen to the sounds of her symphony.

There is no need to think and judge, you can let your worries go with a deep sigh of relief. Mother Nature knows how to unravel your stress in her calm aptitude and can transmute it into renewable energy.

Receive this gift that keeps giving and let yourself be filled with the bounty of goodness. Let yourself be swept along the songlines of nature's symphony.

Earth Shift

The Hopi, a Native American tribe of Northeastern Arizona, U.S.A., are referred to as "The Oldest People" and are widely known for their spiritual beliefs rooted in the natural world. They believe they are caretakers of the Earth who work in respect and union with the sacred balance of Earth's ways.

According to an ancient petroglyph on Hopi land known as Prophecy Rock, it was depicted that the First World was destroyed by fire, the Second World by ice, and the Third World by floods. These worlds were destroyed consecutively as people became greedy, fought and hurt each other, and repeatedly forgot the teaching that was given to honor and respect Earth as a source of life and sustenance.

This Hopi Prophecy stipulates that if humanity does not return to the natural cycle of Earth and live along with her as a sacred living being, that the cycle of destruction will occur again. It speaks of the split of humanity of those who are following the path of the heart, which is connected to Mother Earth's heart, who shall be raised to a higher ground of consciousness, where abundance reigns... And those who follow the path of the mind, of the ego, that shall remain in the mire of lack, war, ravage, and separation.

Another society that reveals similar clues for this plausible outcome is the demise of an ancient civilization known as Atlantis, written about in the classical Greek Athenian philosopher Plato's account of *Timaeus and Critias*. This was an empire where people lived longer and led peaceful lives in a civilization where weapons or conflict were unapparent. It was a highly organized spiritual society at the top of its game, gaining more and more power along with the abundance of material wealth. But as the momentum of power and wealth proliferated, spiritual importance was de-emphasized, and more sight was drawn attention toward power and control through wealth and weapons. This resulted in the degradation of their empire and was depicted by shorter life spans, death, conflict, violence and war. It was said that as punishment, the Gods sent "one terrible night of fire and earthquakes" that caused the island of Atlantis to sink into the sea.

The story of Atlantis and the depiction of Prophecy Rock are signals and clues to not repeat history, but to keep our sight on what is truly important for our greater well-being. We need to swing the pendulum from power, greed, and violence to sharing, caring, and kindness with greater awareness toward preserving our spiritual virtues and sanctity for our future generations. We are now on the cusp of a similar demise if we continue to breach the laws of kindness and reciprocation.

Corruptive systems, where the governing impetus is led by greed and power, are still in place and may seem more pernicious than history has accounted for. But the opposite is true as well, as there is always equal and opposite energy counteracting and balancing any given equation.

Humanity is on the verge of a spiritual resurgence. We are becoming more mindful of how we have trespassed the sacredness of our living planet, and we are slowly but surely becoming more aware of the empowerment of our lives that a righteous path brings. Awareness for a "greener" planet is on the incline as recycling is now implemented in our daily lives, and the momentum to seek natural alternatives to plastic or synthetic fibers has never been higher. Natural sources of wind, solar and hydro energy are more commonly chosen and organic gardening, organic produce and eco-friendly products have become the trend. Where in the past humanity had turned a blind eye to these things, it is now wide-eyed for a more sustainable future.

Spiritual practices such as yoga and meditation have never been as widespread as they were in the past, and life coaching and couples counseling are part of the weekly routine for a more fulfilling and enriching life. The choices are now in place for us to elect a better world, a more sustainable and natural world. A shift is happening, and many know it as the Earth Shift. This is a shift in consciousness; an upgrade to a higher level of operating within ourselves and in humanity. One where we are not looking only for our individual gain and wealth, but the awareness of how our choices impact the greater whole. One where our spiritual life takes precedence over material wealth alone.

All of life is asking for this evolutionary shift. The stars, the planets and the cosmos, too, are assisting in helping us make this change toward a more wholesome and truthful world. Astrologers are witnessing unprecedented and intense stellar configurations that are squeezing the face of humanity, shaping its profile into a more sober countenance as the hard-hitting planets of Pluto, Saturn, Uranus and Mars, each with their own temperaments, play a part in activating and revolutionizing our way of thinking. Together they play a role of unearthing hidden secrets that have operated under the radar of deceit, igniting change, shaking and breaking up the foundations of obsolete establishments of government and of organizations that have kept us compressed under the thumb of power and greed.

The astrological constellations of our times are triggering the breakdown of the old ways of oppression to wave the flag of freedom and to bring in new paradigms, innovative ways of thinking, broader perspectives and new ways of being more spiritually abundant within ourselves. Accelerated light particles released from solar, lunar, stellar, photon and cosmic light all inform our systems to uptake this light—this new energy and the information they bring to us—to speed the adaptation process in order to evolve to higher levels of existence.

It is therefore imperative, more than ever, to take heed of what we have endured in the recesses of our history and listen to the wisdom messages of our ancestor's foresight. It is critical to keep humble and stay in touch with the Earth, for she can balance these incoming electrical forces of energy and keep us grounded to her magnetic field. Despite our neglect and despoilment of the Earth, she remains our loving mother! With that, we can more readily anchor these new forms of light into our nervous systems and into our bodies, putting in positive motion the new change that awaits.

ACTIVATION

Ask yourself how you can contribute to raising the bar of awareness within yourself, of your thinking and of your actions.

What thoughts are you willing to shift in order to propagate a healthier, more abundant life of goodness?

What spiritual practice can you incorporate into your daily life that could lift your spirit to a higher plane?

Bear Encounters of the Shamanic Kind

My association with Bear began in 2006, just after my first book, *Spirit of the Stones*, was printed and ready to be taken out into the greater world. It relays the true account of my psycho-shamanic-spiritual journey and the synchronic events that uncovered an Earth assignment I was to carry out... One that I had started in the ancient past that was now asking me to complete in this current life.

I had spent seven years out on the land with the stone megaliths of Sedona, Arizona, to listen to and retrieve the wisdom of the stone beings and to impart their messages to humanity. In effect, I became the secretary to the Earth. This active prayer in listening and deciphering Earth's wisdom resulted in a book woven with stone retrievals in a most intimate journey with Mother Earth, and my experience was about to become public! I was excited and a little nervous about revealing my deep inner passage that I knew would help others—and in the process, expose myself fully.

By the time I had completed my book, I had been steeped beyond all reasonable doubt in the shamanic realms with countless visions, dreams, and synchronicities all vying for my attention to listen and follow the messages of Spirit. By this stage, I had already been initiated into the realm of the shamanic animal Spirit World by visitations and encounters with the eagle, the owl, and the bee, but had never imagined Bear would or could become significant to me personally. I knew it was a powerful animal spirit, but it was never on the front lines of my awareness as a totem animal by any means until the bear started to come to me in my dreams.

Medicine Dream Bear:

My first encounter with Bear Medicine was in a very powerful and lucid dream-vision that affected me very deeply. I was standing in the direction of the south, facing into the center of a great wheel of stones, into a medicine wheel, with nothing else surrounding but white light. At the center of the wheel was a Great Mother Bear sitting strongly in the power of her claimed space. She was unwavering and very powerful on the throne of "her" domain. I knew she was a mother bear, for she was fierce and very protective of this ground— her space. With great reverence, I very slowly and carefully crouched low on my knees close to the earth and held my newly published book out to her with both extended hands. I was very eager to give it to her and scooched in a bit closer for her to see the book, hoping that she would accept it as a gift from my inner being. I was humbled by the presence of her power and authority and did not dare to make eye contact with her lest I may startle and agitate her. She did not move or budge. In fact, she remained motionless, and I felt that the acceptance of my book was not made.

I proceeded to the west direction of the wheel to approach her from another angle. Once again, I crouched down close to the earth with my head bowed down, extending my arms out to her with my book in hand. This time I took the courage to look up to let her see me, so she could, for a moment, recognize my spiritual and shamanic journey. Patiently, I waited for her to make a gesture of acknowledgment. Perhaps there would be a nod, or she would lift it out of my hands, or something to show she had recognized my plight in bringing my book out to the greater wheel of life... Again, no show or sign of acceptance!

I moved around the wheel once more and as it is in dreams, the unexplainable occurred. Even though I moved around the wheel and would expect to have proceeded to the north position, I remained in the west direction. Once again, and without discouragement, I inched closer this time, bowed my head, and offered my book to her—my life journey with all my heart. She had not moved or faltered in her powerful stance, and I knew this was to be my last and final offer. My heart was to stay pure and untainted from all doubt and I remained there in my purity until I felt her take it from my hands and accept my book like a Great Mother Queen.

As she took my book in her large paws, I felt her fold me into her inner earth lodge, her den of dreams, into the primal feminine, into the Great Mother energy. With her silent wisdom, she showed me that she could not be swayed or persuaded from the Truth and that only those who are worthy and who approached with earnest purity and humility are allowed to enter "her domain."

I pondered and meditated on this dream-vision for a long while over the following months and couldn't overlook that the direction of the west in the wheel was of great significance to me. I studied the Native American way of the medicine wheel and came to know that the west signifies the time of our lives when we begin to make our own decisions and develop our own values. This is the direction where, as adults, we reap the harvest of our endeavors, which symbolically relates to the food harvest we gather in the springtime to sustain ourselves throughout the long sleep of winter.

The direction of the west is depicted by the color black. It represents the inner cave of self and the womb, where we enter to discern what we release and let go of and also begin to conceive what we give birth to. Like the black of night, it requires stillness and quietude to hibernate in the cave of silence to prepare for the next season within. This direction I found was represented by the Great Mother Bear, who can be gentle, protective and also fierce when situations demand it of her.

Bear's visitation in my dream was a portend, teaching me to listen more deeply, to be patient before jumping ahead, to take heed before making brash decisions, and to be humble with how the greater stirring within me moves me around the wheel of life. And on a deeper level the bear was reflecting that part of myself that was asking me to fully accept my gift of self to the world.

Flat-Toothed Bear:

My second encounter with Bear came six months later in another dream-vision I received in Taos, New Mexico, U.S.A., during my book tour that was blessed by the Great Mother Bear in the medicine wheel.

> *I sat in front of a live bear's head that was cut off at the neckline. Animal skin, most likely bear hide, was stretched over the neck to form a drum. I knew with great certainty that it was my drum, my bear drum. Its hair was thick, its eyes were closed, and it felt like it had been hibernating for an eon and that it was I, and only I, who was to awaken it after its long slumber. This one was a big, brown male bear. I stroked his left brow cautiously and gently to let him know that I knew he was my drum so as not to startle him after his long dormant sleep. As soon as I made contact, his eyes opened wide in a flash of an instant. I was startled and astounded by his stark power and strength. His eyes were a forbidding black and I was not expecting the magnitude of his power and jumped back in fright. I braced myself and told myself that this was my drum, that I know how to use it and take charge of it. I took a deep breath and proceeded with caution once more. This time, I was afraid. I stroked him lightly again on his left brow, and once again he opened his eyes with a dark glare that alarmed me. He looked at me with such impersonal power, with no emotional connection and said, "Do Not Be Afraid."*
>
> *All the fearful emotions started to stream in. "I'm not allowed, but I am allowed, this is my drum. I am unacceptable, I am helpless. I am as powerful as the bear and not one iota less, I have awoken the beast and now would not be excused, I*

have activated this massive power that has lain dormant and now what?" I jumped back with just as much fear, no difference from the first time.

In spite of my fear of his formidable presence, I had to give it one more go. It was my drum, after all, and I had to gain some respect from it and for myself. I paused to gather myself and took a few deep breaths to regain my center so that I could start afresh without bringing the fear of his stark power to this next attempt. I summoned my power for this most powerful of initiations. I approached with presence and reverence and shook off my fear. In this attempt to tame my fears, I slowly touched his brow one last time. I knew at this stage that I was only given three chances at this. He opened his eyes fiercely and again I was just as startled, but this time he opened his mouth and gnashed his teeth at me. In a very stern and authoritative tone he said, "I told you not to be afraid. You see, I am a flat-toothed bear, a friendly bear." Then with a snap, I awoke.

His teeth were indeed flat, which revealed a side to him that was less fierce and ferocious; more emotional, with a sense of humor and of compassion than his eyes disclosed. He was, after all, a friendly bear. My friendly bear.

This dream bear was mirroring the significant power that was lying somewhat dormant within me. He was showing me the inner potential and authority that I had been afraid of—and that this power used, along with compassion and humaneness, is not dangerous to others or myself. After all, I am a flat-toothed bear and cannot harm others when revealing my inner fierceness.

Wisdom Bear Encounter of the Third Kind:

A few days had passed when I drove south along the green, flowing river of the Rio Grande to Santa Fe. Since I had published my book, I had not conducted a stone retrieval for quite a while. I now felt the call again to commune with the rocks in this particular region to see what they had to say.

Driving out of the busy part of town into the wilder nature is where I headed. As per usual, I had asked the stone beings to guide me as to where they would like me to perform the stone retrieval. I parked my car at a modest trailhead and walked for at least twenty minutes before I saw any rocks. They were a small crag of rocks only five feet high and three feet wide, located just off the trail. These were unlike the megalithic rocks I was used to tapping into in Sedona, AZ, but were rocks, nevertheless.

I approached with great diplomacy and reverence to begin the stone retrieval. "Greetings, my name is Amalia Camateros and I have come from a far and distant land of Australia to do the Earth Work. I now live in Sedona, Arizona and wish to undergo a stone retrieval. If you deem me humble enough to impart your wisdom, I am ready to receive it."

I addressed and called in the four directions of the East, South, West, and North, along with honoring the Earth and Sky. I took a pinch of tobacco and pollen out of my medicine bag and sprinkled them around the rocks, along with a trickle of water for the plants at the base and also a trickle at the crown of the stones. I began by taking a few long, deep breaths and rested my forehead on the cool rock surface. I was a little rusty but knew how to empty my mind of thoughts in order to make my passage into the stones and waited for their wisdom.

It was only a few minutes when I heard the rocks speak: "We were once a moving tribe of stones." After a few quiet moments, they proceeded to say, "We were once a moving tribe of bears." For a brief moment, I thought, *Uh oh, I have lost the touch, I haven't undergone a retrieval for a long while and now I am losing the pulse of it.* I had to tell myself that my commitment to the Earth Work is not to judge what arises, but to be open to the information that comes through, lest I taint what I was seeing and hearing. I had to trust.

The rocks proceeded to say, "Even though we had individual heads and arms and legs, we were traveling under... ONE BEAR

SKIN!" These last few words resounded like a living echo in my being. I saw the vision of this clear in sight. I was shown a large sleuth of brown bears running in front of me, heading toward my west from right to left. They were running together with arms raised, holding one mammoth bear skin. The stones continued, "A bit like you humans. Even though you have individual heads, your own arms and legs, YOU ARE TRAVELING UNDER ONE HUMAN SKIN!" I was astounded at what I heard and saw and simply could not dismiss the authenticity of this stone wisdom—Mother Earth's wisdom.

I accepted this bear teaching with great humility. "Thank you rock beings for giving me such great wisdom, I receive it fully and completely." I completed the ceremony by breathing deeply into the stones with my love and closed all of the directions, thanked the spirit of the land along with Great Spirit, and quietly left. It was now on the earlier side of getting dark and I thought it best to get a move on as I had a good twenty minutes before I would reach the road where my car was parked. I meandered back to the trail, pondering deeply about such a retrieval and acknowledged myself for not doubting the stones' wisdom but keeping it pure by trusting it all the way to the end of the teaching.

I felt I had accomplished a great feat in reconnecting into Mother Earth's wisdom in this way again and was fully satisfied with this rhetorical and formidable message. Then, I heard the crack of a twig! I looked to where the sound had come from, and what did I see at that very moment? A bear. Yes, a *live* bear!

It was about 100 feet away and going up a small, inclined hill. Even though its body was facing in the direction it was headed, its head was turned back toward me. *How could this be real?* I thought. *I just retrieved a bear wisdom message from the rocks and a bear is right here with me now.* This time, I was face to face with it for real. My heart was racing—pounding, in fact. I stood in all that I had learned from my encounters with Bear and took a few long slow breaths to remain calm and grounded. We both stood there staring at each other without a trace of movement for at least four minutes.

In the thunderous silence and stillness, a single tear welled up in my eye and fell to the Earth. It was in this stark silence that I spoke to Bear. "I am human and you are animal. If there is anything I can do or give to you that may help you in your evolution, I am available and willing to give to you my energy, but you cannot harm me in any way." I stood there with my hands open for the giving of my humanness and all that I had experienced in my life and then spoke again to the bear. "And if there is anything at this time that you want to share with me, of your medicine, of your teaching, I am now willing to receive." I did not blink to shift the energy as one tear slowly formed after the other, dropping into the ground by my feet. Such a profound purity was felt where time had collapsed into yet another synchronism beyond reason or rhyme.

After several minutes of communing with the bear, it simply turned its head back in the direction it was headed and slowly lumbered over the hill. Afterward, I was in absolute awe to have this encounter and spiritual communion with Bear immediately after this most curious of rock retrievals. It was an affirmation that the wisdom I heard and saw was concrete and not imagined. As I have conveyed in my book, *Spirit of the Stones*, the rocks do not speak with us in the ways that we are accustomed to, but rather speak to us in a shamanic way, in a figurative way. All we need to do is to stop, be silent, and listen to Mother Earth speak.

Medicine Grizzly Bear:

It was only a few weeks later when I was giving a workshop at Stewart Springs, in Mt. Shasta, California, where I met a Native American medicine man by the name of what? Medicine Grizzly Bear! He was there to teach the retreat participants about the Native American medicine ways. He held the way of power and stood tall and strong like a bear himself. I approached him with grave anticipation as I knew it is not taken lightly to go and start up a conversation with an elder medicine man, for great respect is at hand. His tradition and name seemed apt for me to take the courage to ask how Bear medicine may relate to me and why it had come into my life so repetitively.

As I came near, I spoke. I was confronted with the same stark fierceness that the bear drum had revealed in my dream-vision. I had been given three attempts to stay in my power in that vision, and now when I was confronted with the same formidable authority, I was able to remain grounded and hold my own power without being taken aback.

While I was telling him my story about my bear encounters, his eyes flashed with that same untethered power that my bear (drum) had revealed in my dream. Fear arose, and I could feel myself contracting and pulling back into my shell, my inner cave where it was safe!

I remembered the sacred bond that I felt with my real live bear encounter right after the rock retrieval and felt my body relax and return to a state of humility and sacred respect. I emitted that energy to Medicine Grizzly Bear and continued to speak, little bear (me) to big bear (him). I asked him to speak of the significance of Bear as he knew it. His stance took on a larger-than-life form, like a bear that had raised itself up on its two hind legs, and he proceeded to impart his wisdom.

"Bear Medicine is strong medicine, very powerful, this is not a medicine to play with as it can attack at any point and shred you to pieces. This is a strong teacher and healer medicine, be aware." Medicine Grizzly Bear's explanation was short and succinct but received in humility. I realized that this was no child's play medicine and that I would have to stand up for it as it may shred me to pieces lest I stand my ground. I was to stay in humility and respect for the power it continued to reveal to me.

To this day, I recognize the primal bear in me. Some call me "mama bear"; in fact, others are taken aback by the power that I can bring to a situation. I am very protective, especially in standing up for the truth. I can comfortably retreat into the cave within, to digest life's tribulations and assimilate them to teach the lessons in the greater wheel of life. I have learned to balance the formidable power of Bear with the gentleness of the feminine spirit and along with Mama Bear, I have been called by the name of Fierce Grace among friends. I will, with loving intent, remind you to be impeccable with your word, to walk your talk, and get off your knees to stand strong in your own power!

ACTIVATION

Which animal keeps appearing in your world of dreams, visions, or encounters? What could this animal be saying, suggesting, or sharing with you?

See if you can decipher what the thread of wisdom is for you and apply it to your life in actuality, in your embodiment, in your truth.

Even if an animal comes to you in your dreams or in waking life, heed its message, the way it moves and lives, as it may be asking you to embody its medicine power.

SHAMAN

I was jolted awake by a startling vision. It was a strong revelatory dream that woke me from a deep sleep that transported me to a world away.

Six large, chunky, bold, block capital letters:
S...H...A...M...A...N floated on the surface of a still ocean. The letters cast a silhouette against the dark gray skies, which set the scene for the formidable teaching I was about to receive.

Each letter was separate and on its own and yet in complete unison, shoulder to shoulder and side to side, in balance, poise and utter silence. They were sitting on the surface of the water, like surfers on their boards, patiently waiting in full presence and readiness—not for a "maybe" moment, but for the perfect moment—for the perfect wave to catch and ride. They waited in reverent silence as they mustered the courage within to meet the unrelenting wave that could swallow them into the great sea.

This dream-vision summoned the teaching that asks us to listen, wait and notice before making our move. It invites us to curtail our senses inward and into the greater capacity of "seeing" in order to respond with full awareness, rather than react out of impatience or the short fuse of agitation that we often move from.

This S H A M A N teaching asks us to watch for the details while garnering a wider perspective through the lens of perception, so that you are not reacting from your momentary impulses, without taking the extra moments to observe the broader, more panoramic view of your experience. This teaching invites you to open the shamanic lens of your senses and listen for the twig that snaps, the rustle of the leaves in the wind, to watch for any distraction that steers you away from Self and to return your wandering eye into the deeper world of nature. Keep your eyes open for the magic that lies underfoot!

The excerpt from my book, *Spirit of the Stones,* is apropos in the conserving and reigning in of our mindfulness here:

> *Sinking down into the soul of the land, deeper and deeper into the stillness of silence. The shaman within us dies to the outer world and summons himself to the Underworld, sinking deeper into his own desolate terrain, curtailing his senses, and redirecting and turning them inward. Little but his own breath is the connecting link to life. He sees, feels, tastes, smells and hears no more, as he has died to the life he knew. All the senses now evolve into one new sense, one of utmost sensuality, sense-you-all-ity, sensing the All That Is. A new landscape is birthed, one where the shaman walks between worlds. In honoring this death, he gives rise to a new spark of life.*

The shaman curtails his senses inward, lest they take him out of his trancelike state of being; a state from which he retrieves the hidden wisdom that he can seize from the unseen world—the world beyond the physical.

Like the surfer S H A M A N's plight, he does not get caught up in the next wave of confusion or turmoil, but rides it with mastery. He knows how to use the full sense of his being while curtailing his senses inward, to conserve his energy, so that when needed, he can capture with clear response the perfect moment in which to launch his power into.

Shamans traditionally positioned and poised themselves at the edge of the tribe, or the village. They are the seers, healers, and medicine men and women who remain on the edge of this reality, with one foot in the unseen worlds of Spirit and the Underworld and the seen Physical world with the next. From this watching, seeing and curtailing their senses inward, they can ride the crest of the wave or the edge of reality to retrieve the unseen messages blind to the ordinary eye. From this vantage point, a shaman can delve into the innermost heart and soul of the tribe for healing and settlement of resolution.

The S H A M A N is tethered and grounded with the Earth like a snake and yet able to soar high into the sky like an eagle. Walking between worlds and on the razor's edge, they are the bridge between the physical and the Spirit World. Here is where they can watch, witness, and wait in the void of distraction for the spark of light and consciousness to guide their way.

Just like the big, chunky, heavy letters that can float on the water's surface, heavy in substance but light in weight, we are invited to remember that we are fully physical in our bodies and yet made of Spirit that has no weight to be measured. We are here and yet not here; we are nowhere and everywhere.

We are S H A M A N.

ACTIVATION

Step out into the natural world or a quiet place and practice being in the world and not of it. Draw your senses inward and go into the quiet space of watching and feeling without being pulled away from your awareness. Sit or stand in the world of the physical, in your body, and be aware in the very same moment that you are made of non-physical—of Spirit.

Allow yourself to be the S H A M A N that lives between the worlds and enter the nowhere and everywhere space that exists within. In this space, listen, watch and feel with poise and balance for the wave of wisdom to arise. Ride it all the way and bring it back to yourself and your tribe for healing and resolution.

Become Your Own
Inner Shaman

We have all the wisdom teachings in the world available to us at all times. Mother Nature provides not only food, a natural pharmacy, materials for shelter, and an adventure playground, but her spiritual council too.

Many clients ask me, "Where did you get your shamanic training? Who was your teacher?"

My answer: "From the greatest teacher and shaman of all time."

"Oh yes, who is that?" they await in eagerness and bated breath.

"From Mother Earth direct. Where else did the original shamans of the world learn it from, but from the natural world around them?"

Shamanism is said to have been seeded in Siberia more than ten thousand years ago, but in my book, it was since the first man walked on Earth with his bare feet on the ground. Earth is our Grand Mother Shamaness, showing us in her very simple, yet profound ways of how to live according to the Law of the Land. She teaches us how to live in right relationship and harmony with the elements we know as Earth, Water, Fire and Air; to honor the ground we walk on, to bless the water we drink, to respect the fire we are warmed by and to revere the air that sustains us.

It is through the elements I have termed the "Agents of Power" that we can observe the wisdom teachings of Mother Earth. Here are some of the ways to decipher her wisdom-ways. The opportunity is there for each of us to interpret the wisdom in the way we receive it at the time:

The Earth element invites us to get out of our busy heads and drop our awareness down into our bodies, into the stability and security of the solid terra firma under our feet. This allows us to regain our footing and stand as sturdy as a tree with our roots in the ground within the constant flux and change of the world around us.

The Water element demonstrates how to let go and flow along the meandering path of life and to soften and smooth out the hardness of our rough edges. It helps us replenish and refresh our wilted sense of self when we may most need it.

The Fire element teaches us to purify ourselves by burning away the intensity of emotions that may no longer serve us for our highest good. It also serves to heat our body and soul when we feel bereft and alone.

The Air element affords us the opportunity to allow the breeze to clear away the inner cobwebs of the mind and to take a deep breath of fresh air, thereby allowing us to let go and surrender our worries and concerns to the highest good. It re-minds us that each new breath offers a new living moment to embrace.

The Ether element gives us the quantum space to have our thoughts and dreams be planted in the field of consciousness. It calls us into becoming the physicalized expression of our greater potential and to experience the vastness of who we are.

This is how the Shaman within deciphers the wisdom of his/her surroundings: to watch, to see, to listen, to feel, to open to how Mother Earth may be speaking to them at any given time. They interpret how the rocks and mountains teach us to watch the spin of the world that surrounds us as we remain firm and still within.

They show us how to not react to what passes by, to not squawk at the dark clouds, the sudden rain or the scorching heat—but instead, to remain present with what passes by with the direct nature of reality within the meditation of life itself. Flowers, and plants too, teach us to face the light of the sun, to look on the bright side of life and to allow the beauty of simplicity to lead the way.

Trees are some of our greatest wisdom teachers and shaman elders of all time. They show us how to stand tall with roots (our feet) connected to the ground, trunk (our torso) upright in strength with respect and integrity of self, and branches (our arms) reaching toward the Sun and the light of Great Spirit. They teach us that much of life that we are unaware of is going on underground, in the unseen world.

This correlates to the part of ourselves that we are often unaware of, that gets pushed down into our deeper interiors, that is often hidden in the basement with the door locked. Behind the door are darker-rooted feelings that run deep—such as fears of abandonment, of not being enough, or that something is wrong with us. This is known in the shamanic healing world as the *shadow self* that needs to be brought into the light of our consciousness for healing and integration.

Trees are shamans alright, as they delve their massive root systems deep into the dark soil, into the unseen, underground, to draw up the nutrients to nourish the higher limbs in the light above.

The work of a shaman is to bring the "unseen" to the "seen," and what we don't fully understand into some cohesive comprehension in our lives. Their service is to delve into the Spirit (the unseen) world, retrieve the message of wisdom, and return it to the tribe, the person, and back to the (seen) world. Thus, they bridge the connection between the spirit and the material worlds.

The correlation between the physical expression of nature and the adaptation to spiritual comprehension is also a shamanic way of being. To take a dive into the deep ocean waters is parallel to taking a plunge into your emotional depths. Or climbing a high mountain peak to see from a higher perspective is analogous to raising your awareness to a higher level.

Like the Shaman, this way of relating to the natural world creates the spiritual bridge between us and our environment, for the root of our shamanic existence is anchored in the lineage of Mother Nature herself.

We each have the capacity to become our own inner shaman when we can STOP and quieten our minds to listen to Mother Earth, listen to her wisdom as she speaks it to us in her silent and most powerful of ways.

Mother Nature roots us in the present, to the ground of our being. She is the power point from which we draw our physical and regenerative energy; right there under our feet on the very ground we stand upon.

She is one of the purest expressions of the All That Is that we have the privilege of experiencing and knowing. Her teachings are universal and embrace all languages and cultures across the board. She is a mother energy that offers her unconditional love to all her children equally and at all times.

Our indigenous ancestors knew this. Not only did they respect and honor the Earth through ceremony, prayer and ritual for their sustenance and provisions, but also for their wisdom and guidance. They revered her as a sacred living being, a living mother, part of their own selves, their greater selves. They showed us how to live in symbiotic harmony and in respectful abidance of the Law of the Land in accordance with the greater circle of all life. They were living shamans learning not from textbooks but from the living library of Earth itself.

We, too, must practice offering our conscious awareness and connect into the presence of this great shaman teacher, Mother Earth, by grounding our minds, by remembering her under our feet and that our heritage and ancestral roots are connected with her. We will not be able to truly see through the eyes of our own inner shaman if our minds are full of electrical activity that is filled with fragmented thoughts. By clearing our mind screens, we are more able to see and decipher the hidden messages before us.

Mother Earth, as a living and loving being, loves to commune with you on this intimate level. She has a plethora of wisdom waiting for you.

The activation below will show you how to clear your mind in order to fully commune and connect with Mother Earth and become your own inner shaman more readily.

ACTIVATION

Step into Nature with wondrous eyes as a child. You remember this feeling—it is still within you. Behold (be and hold) the magic and the wisdom that is available at all times. When entering the state park, the local park or your own backyard, wave your hands down from the top of your head and sweep all the mental thoughts, entanglements and anxiety down to the ground—to Mother Earth—with some long exhales. Do this a couple of times to sync your mind with your body as your sacred self before you enter the sacred space of the Mother.

Find a quiet space to stand like a tree yourself, with your roots in the ground, your trunk tall and your branches high! Become an antenna of light and bridge the world of Spirit and Matter, bridging the light of Heaven into your body and into the Earth. Let go of the tension—the electrical mental energy—by shaking it down from the head to the ground like the dead leaves of a tree. Mother Earth will receive it lovingly and mulch and recycle all that you no longer need into fertilizer, into new energy for your own growth.

Get present. Turn on your shamanic eyes and ears and listen with your present awareness. Walk in wonder, walk in a way of prayer. Let your intuitive side open. See if you can observe what Mother Earth is showing you and listen to what she is saying to you. Feel her presence and wisdom that is often overlooked with the naked eye. Let the first thought be the right one, without manipulating or doubting the message you receive.

SPIRIT

The Spirit section pertains to the inquiry of thought, ideology, and our spirit-soul self. These excerpts loosen our inner programming, raise us to a higher vantage point of observing our humanness, and expand the edges of our conscious awareness.

No Beginning
and No End

At one of his presentations, a prominent Mayan elder spoke about how the Mayans built their pyramids with the ages of evolution in mind. Each layer represents a stage of evolution, starting from the base as the oldest and earliest stage, where time moved extremely slowly and evolution took its time to move forward.

As evolution progressed in consciousness, the next step of the pyramid was built, and then the next, and so on, each representing higher levels of consciousness and a faster momentum of evolution at each layer until the pyramid reached its apex at the pinnacle.

He mentioned that time has begun to spin its momentous wheels faster. Presently, we are now at the apex of the pyramid, so to speak, as reflected in how we experience time speeding past us with unmanageable velocity.

He proceeded to explain that the top of the pyramid is where we harvest the fruits of our hard work. This is the time when we can open to receive the fulfillment of our long-awaited abundance; where what we think and feel shall be delivered right at our doorstep as time has collapsed into the now.

There is nowhere to go now but to the place at the top of our own inner pyramid of Self to enjoy the view from the above place. It is not about sitting on our laurels, but seeing that there is no separation between time and space as it once was in the long recesses of history. We can therefore manifest at a more rapid rate and must become more aware of our thoughts and the power they have to shape our reality.

As I continued listening to the elder's wisdom teachings, the sound of his words began to fade in the background as a visual image appeared in my mind:

> *I was looking down on a colossal radial disk that was filled with a lattice of light woven into a tapestry that represented humanity in its entirety. At the west section of the disk, a wedge of the disk was missing, like a piece of the pie that was cut away. It showed me that there was a gap in humanity that needed to be filled. The fabric of this latticework of light was then stretched over so that the two edges were bought together to close the gap. The words I heard were, "CLOSE THE GAP!" A serpent of light appeared and wove itself in and out of the two edges to sew the tear in the fabric of our human plight.*
>
> *I heard the words, "When the two seams of beginning and end are sewn together ALL will be healed again."*

I was shown this vision from a higher vantage point, perhaps from the top of the pyramid, where we had reached the pinnacle of time and space, with no gap between past and future, no space between the base and the top, where only the presence of now remains.

The serpent of light shows us that we now need to mend the tear in the fabric of our being, to sew the edges of the dualities within that have kept us in separation and disconnected from the entirety of our self and humanity. We need to mend the gap with our internal opposites—the conscious and unconscious mind, the masculine and feminine self, the light and shadow aspects within—so that we may return to our original innocence that is connected with our greater, grander selves.

This vision perspective asks us to lay down our sword in the battle "against the other" that impales and maims us. It is inviting us to refashion the sword into a divine implement that can sew the edges of the opposites and close the gap in our consciousness, and pardon the judgments we've kept hidden behind our crooked smiles.

When we sew together the opposites of beginning and end, of good and evil, right and wrong, of past and present, and of birth and death, it is quite possible that the two hemispheres of our brain could function as one entire lattice of light. We would have one functioning unit of integration, with little or no abyss or gap between the conscious and unconscious mind. This would decrease the time-space continuum between the tides of our thoughts and actions, between day and night, between the seasons, and allow for the flow of life's ease between life and death.

I was given the perspective from the top of the pyramid, where I saw the fray at the edges of the seams where we need to mend our ways back to wholeness. We all need to complete the circle of life, experience the unbroken tapestry and flow in the weave of Oneness.

ACTIVATION

When you find yourself having two minds—one saying one thing and the other saying the opposite—sit in stillness and visualize the two sides coming very close together. Allow the connecting sides to touch and perceive the light of consciousness weaving them together as one complete woven tapestry. Feel the uniformity and admire the entirety of the whole.

The Game of Life

The game of life is not about making more money or living the stress of striving toward a goal or a destination that demands endless expenditure. Rather, it is to invest our time and energy and to yield interest from something more valuable, and that is love.

It has become apparent that the driving force of our evolution in this day and age has become money. The drive toward profit pushes us farther and farther from the Ultimate Truth of Love.

Love itself is non-negotiable. It is not something to bargain with or sell to gain a profit. To receive and to give love does not cost us a penny, but in turn pulls us closer to the richness within, where boundless joy resides. The exchange of a simple gesture, a loving glance, a generous smile, or donating time to help another can fill the empty spaces of the heart of those in need.

In the game of life, we can afford to give more of ourselves and receive the simple, yet rich pleasures that life can bring. To play and enjoy ourselves, to laugh and relax more, to create and explore in the sheer delight of discovering things anew returns us to an innocence that brings with it a fresh approach to living a life more fulfilled. If we approach our lives like we do when we start a new game, with anticipation and excitement, we will be lighthearted, cheerful, and joyful like a child at play.

Remember how playing hide-and-seek was thrilling, or playing dodgeball where all eyes were on the ball to avoid at all costs? Or maybe you pretended you were a rock star, singing on the verandah with your make-believe musical instruments, where joy and the use of your imagination filled your attention to no end?

The power of this innocence becomes encumbered over time with the limitation of what life "should look like" in our adulting years. The word "adulterated," after all, begins with the word "adult." The inner child within us is still intact and has never left us, has never left the garden, and still awaits our return. It holds the keys to knowing how to take things lightly and show us how to express the abounding joy from within. As we turn our attention back to our inner child, we are reminded of how it is to play, laugh, be silly and get creative. It is integral to lighten up and feel the carefreeness of our inner freedom.

Many of us spend most of our time working, driven by the notion that the more money we make, the more freedom we have access to. The word *freedom*, however, begins with the word "free," which could give us a clue—a tip, so to speak—that it does not require money to buy or attain it. Freedom can be accessed through Love; the love of our authentic inner child (like nature), and through the love of life itself.

The game of life does not have to entrap and entangle us in the web of the constraints of society. Like any other game, we are asked to abide by the rules, but we can always remember to approach it lightheartedly and with the carefreeness and innocence of the inner child within.

ACTIVATION

Reach into your deeper reserves. How much can you afford to give from the unlimited supply of your spirit? Offer a generous smile, a loving gaze and an inspiring notion to those around you to see how you can spread and multiply your riches.

The Return

In right mindfulness, we are in a constant reach toward the light. Like trees, we are tethered to the ground of Earth and simultaneously strive to reach the greatest heights of Heaven.

Along this growth path, some of us crawl, some leap and bound, some take large detours that take them on circuitous journeys, and others are slow and steady with a keen eye on the goal to win their race. No matter what speed or path we choose, all roads lead to the "return path home"—to the light, back to God, to the Oneness of All That Is.

We are homeward bound, walking our path with an inner knowing that we will, at the end of our journey, be welcomed in the arms of the Divine, into the fold of love and peace, however many revolutions around the Sun and however many turns of the karmic wheel from one lifetime to the next. Many of us as teachers, wisdom guides, coaches, and therapists have also made it our mission in service to guide others along the path, to assist in clearing their lifeline toward unconditional love of Self to Source.

We each have a point at the center of our internal compass that resides in our heart, guiding us home. Home to the One, the omnipresent sentient beingness that streams light and love endlessly into and from our heart. Not from our brain, not from our eyes, but from our heart at the center of our being.

The generating pulse with each beat of our heart re-minds us of this abiding journey toward the greater Love. It does not require an on-and-off switch but operates as an eternal stream of living consciousness. It is a living turbine that streams pure energy through the heart to not only keep us alive, but to synchronize us with the pulse of existence.

We are already self-activated and self-actuated. We need not strive to become something we already are. We are connected to Life in its greater workings through this bio-electro-magnetic currency of living energy at all times, and yet can easily take this for granted and forget the power of this living force that perpetuates our existence.

As we squander this legacy by putting our faith and reliance on external power sources of cell phones, computers, of material gain and wealth, of the need "for more," we risk becoming more mechanical and robotic in nature. The reliance on a "pseudo source" of energy that is outside of ourselves makes us pay dearly for the cost of our living. We have forgotten that the All That Is—God in the Oneness of Creation—is the infinite power source that we operate from, regardless of whether we believe it or not. Every molecule, atom, electron, and proton has, at its very core and center, this generating light that is connected to the higher zenith of an eternal creational source of power.

This is the great Promise that always has been and will always be. We need not compromise ourselves by failing to remember to validate this gift that keeps on giving. To live our lives as a true hero's journey takes us through the myriad of trials and tribulations over lifetimes, allowing us to return home within ourselves, changed and transformed. No, this is not a promise to become complacent about or to take advantage of, but instead to live it in fascination, in deep reverence and respect for the ultimate gift of Life.

Our integral and essential nature knows the long and winding road on our return path home, to the resting place, to rest in peace in the Oneness with the All That Is, no matter how long it takes or how circuitous the journey. It beckons us to this place of rest between each heartbeat that is ever-present within our very selves along our life paths.

Let us not have to die in the physical to rest in peace. Let us rest in the eternal nature of peace in each moment of now and with each heartbeat while we are alive and well.

ACTIVATION

Close your eyes and look within to the place of stillness, to the point of light at the center of your being in your heart center. Take a moment to sense and re-cognize the pure radiance of this God-force, of eternal love, moving to and from your heart with every pulse. Give gratitude for its benevolence, for its Light, its Love, and its Life. Connect into the place of knowing your return path to the Oneness, of All That Is.

The Temple Within

We are each a living temple that houses our soul. A house of God, so to speak. I'm not just referring to the physical nature of our bodies, but the interiors of the mind, the heart, and soul.

A temple is not just a building made of stone and mortar, but the altar at the heart of the temple—the prayers, the chants, the reverence and devotion to the holy sanctum within—is what constitutes a temple. We are a sacred and divine temple of all that we have come to be through our lifetimes and life experiences. We are living proof of the miracle we each and every one of us are. If only we could all feel it enough to know the intrinsic value of the holy house we dwell in. We would treat ourselves as sacred, honoring every action as a sacrament and every utterance as a sacred decree.

In our disposable lifestyles, we have become too busy to go within, carelessly overlooking the holy being that each of us are. We are towers of light, but far too often rely on the outer scaffolding that our egos have built to keep ourselves upright. In our feeble attempt to give ourselves more credence to how we look, and how we want others to see us, we identify with this scaffolding and uphold our disingenuous masks to the outer world.

We tend to reach outwardly for validation and support for the green light; the nod; the stamp of approval. We forget to turn inward to pay homage to the One that resides in the silence within.

We would rather chatter mindlessly, distract ourselves by watching television and videos, or fritter away our time on the computer. We desecrate our temple with substances that numb our senses and debase and vandalize our sacred space with little or no boundaries to protect our holy temple within.

Don't hide the beauty and the intricacies of your deeper sacred self behind the scaffolding that your ego has you propped up in. Let us not only see your façade, but show us more of the depth of your beauty within.

Let us come to know more of you. Let us kneel at the altar of your being. It is time now that we all re-cognize our soul and the intimate relationship we can have with it.

Our soul has guided us all along. It is our inner GPS, globally and infinitely positioning us for our highest good at all times. It nudges us along the higher road, constantly directing us to our True North that directly aligns us to our Higher Self and back to our own soul's intent.

We can stand as towers of light without the outer struts that keep us temporarily upright and erect. Like mighty trees, we can plant our feet and roots in the ground, our trunk upright, strong and sturdy, and our leafy branches reaching for the Light. Like the mighty trees, we can let the light shine all the way down into us, stand on our own, and yet be connected to the greater forest of humanity as a whole.

It is vital that we not only reach for the light, but also keep our temple clean and sanctified, by clearing the blockages that shield the light from shining in and through us.

We can use our higher soul perspective from the tops of our leafy branches to observe from the greater vantage point to see where we hardened and braced ourselves from receiving the light and flow of life. When we do this, we can honor the hardness in its purpose to protect us, which then serves to soften it with compassion.

It helps to take time to come back and pay homage to our inner altar, to our quiet heart space to settle in and re-nourish, re-calibrate, to re-turn home into the quiet temple within, to the holy within.

The ego that requires the scaffolding, with its conniving and manipulative ways, cannot subsist in this pure place of our holy temple.

ACTIVATION

Make the heart space a familiar and comfortable home for you to return to when you have strayed too far away from yourself. Watch with your soulful eye to witness when it is time to release the scaffolding, to stand on your own merits of self-worth. Clear your body temple space so that the light of love can be fully received and your inner shine emanates freely from a place of abundance.

Presents vs. Presence

We each have thoughts and ideas of what we would like to bring forth into our lives. We dream of a beautiful home, more travel to faraway and exotic places, better health, and a loving partner.

We are human, and it is important to dream and feel the longing in our hearts. It is a part of our purpose in evolution to manifest our hopes and aspirations into creation.

The Universe is in full compliance and flows with our every thought as we move from one idea to the next. This was shown to me many years ago when I sprained my ankle severely and was immobile for several weeks. Being a "natural woman," I didn't take any painkillers and utilized this time for inner healing and quiet contemplation, so there were many moments of depth and silence that I was immersed within.

One afternoon as I was sitting in quiet meditation, I was shown something. I don't know who or what was showing me, but this is what I saw:

A point of light symbolic of a thought streamed out from the right side of my forehead and traveled seamlessly in a right angle and stopped to the left in front of my eyes. I was made aware of an invisible fabric that was naked to the visible eye and yet was clearly responding to the thought. It was as if the thought was a thread in the weave that was pulling the fabric into itself. This thought, like a commander, had credence and the Universe responded to its presence immediately without judgment or faltering to make this thought manifest.

This instructive teaching then showed me another point of light, symbolic of another thought, which traveled from that point of light into the opposite angled direction to the right. It happened again: this invisible, clear fabric responded with full consciousness into this next point of thought/light. It was clear and simple with no preference, no resistance, but a pure response to Thought itself.

Physicists have called this the "field,"—an invisible fabric of the Universe where consciousness is said to reside—a field where we can plant our seeds of thought for manifesting outcomes. We are given full access to this field at all times, with no mishap or mistake and no preference as to who has more access than another. We are farmers of our own lives. We can till the soil of existence and grow our yielding crop.

I was shown, in this stillness, just how powerful each thought is and just how vital our relationship is to the greater conscious field. The Universe is listening and responding to our thoughts at all times! It is present with us and we must be present with it as well. We must choose our thoughts wisely with respect to the power each thought has, for each thought has the authority to produce its respective outcome. It is important to keep our thoughts clear and uncluttered so as to allow the universe to answer promptly and at light speed.

We have a tendency to complicate this simple process of thought/action. We place positive affirmations on top of complicated routes to our intentions. We place ladders to the attics of our mind and ropes that swing from one idea to the next. Admittedly, our lives have sped up with pressures that build to a point we cannot sustain. Where once we could say that our mind is like a ping-pong match, with the arguments of thoughts switching back and forth from one side to the other, we can now say that our mind is like a pinball machine, shooting and striking in all directions at once. Our lives have become more complicated, and our thoughts have become more convoluted. Our thoughts, as a consequence, are no longer simple and easy to respond to but rather a complex lattice that actually conceals our most simple desires. We can become lost in the field of dreams that is no longer a field of action.

Not only do we layer one thought upon the other, but we have the tendency to pack our thoughts into a box, wrap up the box with colored paper, and then tie a ribbon in a big bow. We endlessly package our thoughts with ribbons of expectations of how our manifestation or dream will appear and when. We admire the package, all wrapped and shiny, forget our brilliant ideas are boxed within, and think, "It is done!"

We become so enamored by "what we ourselves have created" and hold it so tight in our mind that we forget to send this parcel of hope out into the Universe, where the realness of this manifestation occurs. Our ideas, hopes, and dreams are buried in the tombstones of the mind and are no longer available to be exposed into the light of day, to be freely fulfilled by the Universe.

How do we open up to greater outcomes?

Untie the ribbon, pull the wrapping paper off, and open the box. Let the ideas aerate. Release the thoughts into the ethers of time and space and hand them over to the Universe to take care of.

Perhaps, if we slow down a little and allow one clear idea to be felt and transmitted at a time—rather than changing our mind from one idea, one thought to the next—our well-made manifestation could be delivered to us in Godspeed.

Rather than controlling the outcome, *the presentation of the present*, let go and plant your thoughts into the fertile field where the seeds of your presence can be planted, watered, and sprouted into the light of day and into the light of consciousness. Let the greater unfolding happen.

We are heard, we are responded to, and we are connected more than we know.

ACTIVATION

Practice simplifying your thought process. Like a farmer, plant your seeds of intention in well-aerated soil by pulling out and releasing the extra weeds of thought that complicate your mind field. Become more aware of and exercise the relationship you have with the Universe and its willingness to comply with the command of each and every thought. Choose your thoughts and send them off more intentionally from a place of presence rather than creating a stockpile of undelivered presents.

Shadow Cocoon

Most life forms develop within an enclosed receptacle such as a cocoon, a pod, a shell, or a womb, from which they grow in the confines of safety until they are ready to emerge. There is a period of time in which incubation takes place before the breaking out of the shell or the breaching of the womb occurs. A container is absolutely needed in order to protect what is developing inside until it hatches or births and is ready to withstand the outer elements of its environs.

In a harsh and glaring world, we often prefer to remain in our cocoons—our shells of protection—knowing too well that there will be a time near when we will be summoned to emerge. From the hiding place of our shadows into the light of conscious awareness, from the safety of the known into the unknown, and from a state of contraction and smallness into expansion and bigness that awaits, we must leave the safety of "our shell." The cocoon is just the shell, the encasement. It is the seed, not the plant; the womb, not the baby.

Fear would have us afraid to leave the safety of our emotional cocoons, wanting to stay in the confines of limitation to protect ourselves. The more we remain in these confines, just like Stockholm Syndrome, the more we come to identify with and feel relatively safe in this imprisonment. We may come to identify with our cocoon (the shell of our skin) as who we are, such as our bodies and our faces, and lose sight of that being inside, which needs to hatch and emerge into our greater selves.

Twenty years ago, I received a pivotal phone call from Rabbi Gershon Winkler, a very wise man with great humor, author of more than a dozen spiritual books, and teacher to many. I had met him only briefly at a New Millennium event in 2000 in Sedona, AZ. He was greatly moved by a sacred dance prayer that I offered for the event. We had barely said hello, but he made a point of connecting with me to ask if I could offer a shamanic dance program at one of his retreats at the Walking Stick Foundation. I had only been in the USA for a brief term from my home country of Australia, and I was feeling the pressure of how I was going to be able to stay in the country for a longer period of time. At the beginning of our call he asked me how I was, and I proceeded to tell him how worried and anxious I was about my pending immigration status. There was a moment of silence where I knew he was going to deliver something of great importance...

He said, *"Amalia, focus on your hatching, not on your eggshell breaking."*

I was completely struck by this depth of wisdom, which reached deep within the interior of my shell and stirred some movement from the frozen state I was in. It sent me straight to the within place that needed attention, not on the shell of my existence!

In our developed narcissism as a whole, where our focus is squandered on our vanity and the appearance of the physical rather than the modesty of our spiritual selves, we have been programmed to worship our body as the Self. We have lost sight of our inner knowing that what we are inside is in constant emergence that reveals the truth of who and what we are. Our ego, which initially protects us from feeling physical and emotional pain in our early childhood years, has taken a higher seat of importance. It has started to overly concern itself with its own well-being, thus covering the truth and light of who we truly are!

Our innermost being requires gestation time for development. Yes, it needs protection, but not at the expense of its own emergence.

"The change inside the chrysalis is slow and gradual. The caterpillar's body digests itself from the inside out. The caterpillar is attacked by the same sort of juices that it used in its earlier life to digest food. Many of the organs are hidden in the caterpillar, and they take a new form within the chrysalis. The old body is broken down into imaginal cells but not all the tissues are destroyed. Some old tissues pass onto the insect's new body. One imaginal disk will become a wing, and there are imaginal disks that form the legs, antennae, and the other organs of the butterfly." (Asa Jomard, "What Happens Inside the Chrysalis of a Butterfly?" Sciencing.com, Sciencing, November 22, 2019, https://sciencing.com/happens-inside-chrysalis-butterfly-8148799.html.)

We could say here that the ego is the "juice" that is used in earlier life to "digest the food" of our own experiences. It is also the excrement that can be utilized as a fertilizer to help us transfigure and transmorph into our adult selves. From the caterpillar of our own self-judgment and inadequacies, we can transform into our butterfly selves—into light beings—with less density to hinder our movements as we lift our wings to fly into our freedom-self.

In a sense, we can say that our Ego has covered up the light of who we truly are to protect us from the intensity of truth and radiant beauty. We are in the transfiguration process from caterpillar to butterfly and evolving into the great Earth Angels that we are: angelic beings on planet Earth here to be of service to the greater mankind, to the greater kind of man. If we identify with our shadow that keeps us confined in the darkness of our cocoons, we may sabotage our plight of flight, or our full potential of our light-being selves.

Several years ago in Hawaii, I was invited to massage a visiting guru from India. It was assumed to be a high privilege to even touch him, let alone massage him, but I kept my cool—my humility—in a grounded posture and professional stance. During the session, I heard my Higher Self ask a question, "Amalia, what is it like massaging the guru?"

My first response was, "Massaging his body is awesome. No tension, like plasticine, with pliability like a newborn baby, wide-eyed and innocent in the body of his being..." And then I realized that there was something deeper in the answer that was lying there patiently to be heard...

"*It is not the body; the body houses the spirit.* If I walk into a house and start stroking the walls and identifying the walls of the house as the person's being, I am missing the mark."

Very simply, massaging his body was not massaging *him*, but his spirit. I learned that we cannot continue to worship the body as the being. Yes, it can be a reflection of the inner being, how we treat it and how we feed it, but something else much greater is prevalent. There is a being that lies within that is emerging out of its limited form, out of its hidden self, out of its cocoon into the freedom and beauty of the butterfly being.

> "*What the caterpillar believes as the end of the world,*
> *the butterfly knows as the beginning.*"
> —**RICHARD BACH**

ACTIVATION

Take a few moments in quietude to see and feel what is deep within that wants to be hatched and birthed into the light of day. Take time to get to know the one within that still feels it needs to shelter itself in a shell of protection. Give it gentle permission to steadily grow within its safe encasement until it naturally breaks its shell with ease and naturality.

The Puppeteer of
Consciousness

Sigmund Freud discovered that the subconscious mind is like a storehouse for repressed desires, memories and beliefs that lay dormant within us, but still affect our thought processes, behaviors and actions. This part of the mind cannot be easily accessed by our own will or brought to the surface consciously or deliberately, it requires a deeper submersion to enter its terrain.

A common neuromyth we are very familiar with purports that the general populace only uses 10% of their brain capacity and that the remaining 90% is untapped.

The example of an iceberg is often used to substantiate this, where what we see of the entirety of it is only the top 10%, with the remaining 90% unseen below. This percentage could also indicate the relative gap in conscious awareness between the conscious and the subconscious mind. Like the iceberg, the peak that is seen above the waterline symbolizes the conscious mind, and the humongous body underneath the water represents the subconscious mind, the part of the mind we don't consciously use or see. This could then explain why we see the differential behavior between what we think and consciously wish to say and do, and what we actually feel and react to.

Our subconscious mind is in its primary development phase in the first seven years of our lives. In these formative years, a child, like a sponge, absorbs everything around it, soaking in thoughts, ideas, assimilating feelings, and eventually becomes imprinted by its family dynamics and environs. As it navigates through its early years into its oncoming adult years, the primary foundational state of the child begins to show signs of adulteration, with tinges and blemishes of discouragement and fear. The child begins the arduous journey of growth and challenge, of shadow and duality.

As the discomfort levels of disapproval, abandonment from busy working parents, sibling rivalry, parental arguments, and more serious abuse factors escalate, the child begins to feel unsafe, unaccepted, and unloved. These feelings are difficult to process and integrate at such an early stage of development, which set off survival strategies in order to cope with the pressure of these ensuing and unresolved feelings. More often than not, the child's unconscious strategy creates a split from the pain that is too much to bear and files these difficult feelings back into the records of the subconscious mind. Quickly and steadfastly, the "false face"—the masks of approval of pleasing or putting on a happy face or a cloak of rebellion or disassociation—becomes the norm, and the natural innate authenticity slowly but surely gets buried deeper into the unseen self.

The subconscious mind is very powerful, as it records the treasury of our emotional data. It can be considered as the "puppeteer" that pulls the strings of awareness back into itself, to be noticed, reminding us that there are hidden jewels we need to excavate from the dark soil of our consciousness.

I remember the day I was three years of age:

> *My family often took long walks through the neighborhood on a hot summer afternoon. I was wearing my favorite white tulle dress with lace on the sleeves and a high bodice. I felt very special in it with the feeling of newness, but something was wrong. Something was interfering with this feeling of being in my "best-look dress." I remember looking down to see if something had happened to my beautiful dress. Why was I feeling uneasy? I found the answer: I was strapped into a white leather harness that felt hard and harsh against the softness of*

my dress. It was put on me to keep me safe and in check so I would not suddenly run off onto the road. This happened over a period of time along many neighborhood walks, and even though I understood from the beginning why they kept me on a leash, I felt confined and held back. After all, I was a spirited little girl, very curious and free minded from the beginning. The more I leaped forward to step into the beauty of the trees, plants, and feel the freedom to walk on my own, the more I was pulled back.

In my adult years, when taking strides to move ahead, to take a few steps toward the outreach of my endeavors, I had often felt trapped, held back, and "not allowed" to proceed or succeed. After years of asking the question, "What is holding me back?" I followed the lead; the tether; the leash to my subconscious mind alerting me, "Don't go too far ahead! Stay *back* where you are safe." The memory of the harness helped me understand the reason why I felt held back in my life.

Similarly, the more we try to move or push forward with the mask of confidence, accompanied by the resistance to feeling what feels uncomfortable "back there," the more those strings can pull on us from behind, asking us to take a look back into the dark corridors of our mind to shine the light on what is hidden there, into the stored latent fear and hesitation. It is vitally important to turn around to see what we have buried from the lurking past, what we have held prisoner in the dungeon of our minds. It is necessary to dig up and excavate the dark coal of the past to unearth diamonds hidden down deep in the unseen realms and access the remaining 90% of our mind.

It is not of habitual nature to look "back there" as our society would have us look forward, get ahead, put on a happy face, don't rock the boat, and be positive in order to be socially accepted. In the prehistoric era, our reptilian brain would not have us look back, but instead run from, hide, or fight against the saber-toothed tiger in order to survive at all costs. We are often tethered to something that keeps us trapped in the past, like an old phonograph record that keeps spinning around the axis of pain, where the needle of existence continues to skid back into the groove of that scratch in the record of time.

Similarly, an elephant that is chained to a post discovers that it is unable to break free. Over time it becomes restrained and entrained in its resolve to leave the post and consequently arrests its efforts to walk away. Even when the chain is eventually released, the elephant remains restrained.

The "gap" or chasm we must traverse in order to reach the shore of the subconscious mind is a feat in itself. Taking a dive into the abyss, into the gap of the unknown, into the Void of Self is a courageous undertaking. Turning our awareness back into the hidden realms to look lovingly behind the mask that has fit us so well and served us for so many years—and shine the light of awareness into the darkness of those blind spots—is often terrifying. We each have experienced something painful and traumatic that made us split off from our true selves, our innocent selves. Eckhart Tolle calls this the pain-body. In shamanism it is known as our shadow self, and in psychology as the trauma wound.

How do we look back into the subconscious, where discomfort resides? How can we set ourselves free from the chains of our past?

We can revisit the incident of the trauma-trigger to give solace to that inner child that felt unsafe, rejected, and invalidated. We can reach that little one within us who has shrunken and recoiled in the alone place, who feels not good enough, unlovable, ashamed, and even guilty for thinking it was the cause of "the problem." We can exercise courage to take a deeper look, to coax the wounded part out from the shadows, and let it know that it is safe. Let it know that you *see* it, welcome it, and that you love it, no matter what! Console it as you would your own child or a loving friend. Accept these wounded parts without judgment and invite them into the arms of love.

We simply cannot afford to continue to stuff our emotions down with food, to use sexuality, drugs, or any type of addiction or distract ourselves with excessive buying and social media to avoid our past. Nor can we continue to expect others to fill the gap of emptiness in our psyche.

You are the only one in the universe who knows how to love that part of yourself, just as you are the only one who knows what you experienced. We tend to treat ourselves the way we were treated back then, so if you were invalidated or verbally or physically abused, then you are likely to invalidate and put yourself down constantly or condemn yourself for not being good enough. If you were neglected as a child, then you will most likely put others first before your needs are met. These split-off parts, our shadows, are like orphaned children who long to come home to a warm and safe place. They need to be loved and accepted. It is time to clean out our attics, to call back our spirit, and the energy that was held frozen in time needs to be thawed out with the warmth of our love.

How do we love the "unlovable"?

The first step is to turn your sight inward and shed the light of your consciousness into the darkness of your subconscious. Take a look at what is hidden there. Is there an image that may be symbolic of the pain? What is the color of this energy? What shape does it take form in? Or perhaps you see your inner child? How old are you? Where are you? What is your little self feeling? Observe and witness the feeling with gentleness, kindness, love, and compassion. Just be still and sit with this child, hold it in your loving arms, and make sure it knows you are there in love and safety.

The child's nervous system may not have been able to digest and assimilate the feelings back then, but you can certainly help it now by feeling them in the present moment.

Ask this inner child what it needs. It may reply with, "I just want to be loved," or, "I need to be accepted," or, "I need to feel safe."

Become the loving parent that tells it what it needed back then. Let your inner child know that you are here to take care of it now. Give it what it has always longed for: to be listened to and heard, loved and accepted, and encouraged as the most important person in the universe!

This process reroutes the neural pathway of the brain's network to fire off new nerve cells. In 1949 Canadian neuropsychologist Donald O. Hebb, known for his work in the field of associative learning, coined the phrase, "Neurons that fire together, wire together!" This axiom reveals that every experience, thought, feeling and physical sensation triggers thousands of neurons, which form a neural network. Repeating a thought or experience over and over triggers the same neurons each time, which gets hardwired into our brain's networking system, making it even more difficult to break a pattern and release it. As we re-feel, let go and re-create new thought patterns, we forge new neural pathways with the feelings we are inviting in as our new living reality.

Children, like our subconscious, pull on our strings to get our attention. They make their needs known, and if they are not met, they will yank at your skirt or trousers until they get the attention they need. And if you do not take heed and give them that presence, they yank harder, get louder, or break something until they feel heard. Worse still, if they are not given notice, they may recede and recoil into the background of their own lives. So, the next time your inner child starts to show signs of discouragement and pulls on your fabric of being, don't let your subconscious pull the strings back and keep you strung like a puppet. Turn inward and give yourself a moment to listen to its murmurings. You are the only one in the entire universe that knows exactly what your inner child needs and craves.

It is critical to retrieve the lost parts of ourselves we have left behind in our painful past. They contain a storehouse of energy that was trapped and can now be utilized to move forward in a more conscious state of awareness. Let us give a warm, safe home to the inner orphaned children we have forgotten about. We can give them a home in us as we re-parent, re-present them, and give them a safe, warm place to allow the love and aliveness lying dormant within them to re-emerge.

ACTIVATION

In your daily life, when you are triggered back into those same old feelings of fear and shame, rejection or insecurity, place your loving hand on your heart and address the inner child that feels alone, forsaken, afraid, or lost. Let it know you have got its back, that you are here to protect it. Reassure your inner child that everything is going to be okay and that it is never alone. Have a dialogue with this innermost precious part of yourself, listen to what it needs and desires. Be the loving parent it has always longed for.

The Seesaw Effect

I came to know the significance and power of balance playing on a seesaw when I was just five or six years of age. I had a swing and slide in my own backyard that I became very practiced in, but not this playground equipment. It was in a park just down the street from where I lived, and little did I know the kind of relationship I would have with it. I not only wanted to have fun with it, but I was eager to study and get to know all about it. I was highly intrigued.

It was the first time I had absconded from home to do anything of my own intention and free will. My mother was having her afternoon nap and my sister was at school. I was bored and wanted to go out and play, when I decided to go around the block to where the park was. I was feeling "my own self," enlivened in making a decision of my own accord and thrilled that I was pushing the edges of my reality.

When I arrived at the park, I was the only one there at the time. That is when I saw the seesaw and ran to it. I had not been on one before so had no reference as to how to play on it. I took a moment to figure out how to play on it by myself. I ran to one end of the seesaw that was on the ground, sat on it, and tried to give it a jump-start with my legs to lift it off the ground. But after several attempts, I realized that was not going to work. I then eagerly went to the other end, tiptoed to reach the top and pulled it down to see if it would behave any better. But the same thing happened on that side, and I wasn't sure how to work it.

Being a pretty smart and determined child, I stood and looked at it for a moment and thought, *There must be a way I can play on this thing.* I soon figured that if I stood at the midpoint, the fulcrum point at the center, then I could finally make it swing up and down the way it looked like it was supposed to.

I climbed up to the center point of the apex. To start with, I had to push down hard on one leg to move the wooden plank. As a consequence, it would come down with a hard thud. Then I had to push down with all my might with my other leg to get the other side to move the other way, but again it came down with a hard and loud thud. The left leg had its turn and then the right, and each time the seesaw landed with a thud!

This wasn't much fun after all, but I was dedicated to finding a way that worked. I figured that if I didn't push my legs down so forcefully, I could control the seesaw so that it wouldn't thump down so hard and send a shudder through my body.

I continued to sneak away to the park to get back on the seesaw, only when my mother was having her afternoon siesta. Otherwise, I would not have been allowed to go on my own. I was enthralled by this venture, as that was the only thing I remember that gave me great joy at the time. In fact, it became my point of study, with absolute clarity and knowing that I was to work on *how* to bring the seesaw into perfect horizontal balance and absolute stillness, with me at the center of it! Why, I wasn't sure, but that was the agenda.

Over the span of the next few weeks, I would climb up to the middle of the seesaw and practice again to get that plank straight and still. It took all of my concentration to focus on using my thigh muscles to control the wooden plank so that what I did on one side, I had to counterbalance on the other. What I noticed is that if my focus was distracted by even one mere thought such as, *Oh look at me, I am getting it!* or, *How long have I been here? Is my mother worried about me?* the plank would rudely tip to one side, and I lost all the hard work I had put in to come to some semblance of balance.

This took a lot of my effort. Nothing in my life took that much energy up until that point, and I was enthralled with this new priority in mastering the seesaw.

I learned that I had to keep clear of any thoughts whatsoever. If a thought *did* start to arise, I could quickly bring my attention back to my focus to restore the balance once again.

I was ahead of the game now. After several more weeks, I was able to lessen the sway on either side; I was getting close. I am not sure what I was hoping for, but perfect balance and stillness were my aim.

I remember the momentous day that it happened! It involved so much concentration on my behalf to be "one with the seesaw"; to be able to move it incrementally on either side of its midpoint. During that one instance when I *got it*—when the plank came into complete balance in the still point—it was like a switch had been turned on. There was a silence, a stillness, an openness, an emptiness, a fullness in an undivided presence. It was a wholeness so Absolute that it filled me with undivided freedom, filling my entirety with a blinding white light that dissolved the me that I knew.

It was in this still point—this zero point where the duality of movement that swung from side to side, from effort to ease, from up and down—had arrived at the center of all things. Right there between the dualities is where the stillness of ease exists. There are no thoughts, no concerns, no angst, no me and no them. I had entered what I now have found to be called a state of Nirvana or Samadhi, a state of profound equanimity, luminous mind and liberation from respective suffering. I had found something amazing, miraculous; I had found the true state of me, the unlimited me, the All That Is me.

As I continued to practice standing on the fulcrum—on the edge of reality—right there at the center point, I started to study it and get really good at it, where I could enter this middle realm between the dualities regularly. I also came to realize why this playground equipment is called the "seesaw." Because when you are up on the high end, you "see" from the above place, and when you are down on the low end, you "saw."

I now call this the "Seesaw Effect." It has since become an integral part of my healing, teaching, and spiritual work. I use this technique with my clients and students to illustrate how to get into your center (not on an actual seesaw, but creating the effect of moving their arms slowly and consciously up and down on either side of their torso like a seesaw, keeping the arms straight like a plank of wood until they incrementally arrive to the "straight plank" into a standstill at the horizontal line at the heart level).

When we stand at the center point of the duality of our conflicted thoughts and indecisions, we can reach the still point where the body and mind become one, where we can be in the stillness and entirety of self. Here is a place that offers us clarity and balance to arrive at a more whole place of choice.

Right there where the heart lies is the heart of the matter; at the still point of the pendulum swing where the polarities meet, where positive and negative become one, is where the light of the infinite awaits. May we keep our mind and heart open to the simple experiences we receive in the playground of life that may just become the most enlightening teaching of all.

ACTIVATION

Stand with legs shoulder width apart, and keep your torso and head in center alignment. Keep your arms absolutely straight like a plank of wood on a seesaw, with one up toward the sky and the other down toward the earth.

Start to move your arms up and down very slowly on either side of your torso. Each time you lower one side, the other moves in unison in the opposite direction. Each time you change from earth to sky and from sky to earth, you are lessening the arc incrementally.

Keep breathing and stand straight. It is important to keep your torso still like the fulcrum point of the seesaw, while your arms move up and down. Like a straight plank, they are moving uniformly a little less on each side, coming closer and closer toward the midpoint between earth and sky, your arms outstretched as they finally arrive at the horizontal plane across the heartline.

Stay present, and feel this meeting, this moment of zero-point energy. Notice how still and quiet your mind is and what awareness this brings to your attention.

You can use this exercise whenever you feel off-kilter or imbalanced. It only takes a few moments and will bring you much peace of mind.

Dance of Light
and Shadow

We are living in a dimension where not only time, space, and depth have strong roles to play in our reality, but Contrast and Duality play a strong part too. It is Contrast that entrusts the dynamism of one-from-the-other, as one polar rendition coexists with its opposite pole in order to support its entirety.

Positive and Negative, Sun and Moon, Above and Below, Electric and Magnetic are all superstars of this expression. For how can we know day without night, expansion without contraction, stillness without movement, and silence without sound? The two go hand in hand, like two faces of the same coin. They belong together in holy matrimony as does inhalation and exhalation, as does life and death. One is not better than or trying to outshine the other, but rather compliments it in full respect for each to shine on the stage of life equally.

We are versed in the knowledge that opposites attract and that the same poles on a magnet put together can repel each other no matter how hard we try to connect them. But connecting opposite poles will, however, affix them with ungovernable force. The more the polarity, the more the magnetism.

We have also applied this rule of thumb to the equation in our relationships, especially our significant others in the maxim, "opposites attract." It is most likely that we are magnetized and charmed by a partner who illustrates contrasting characteristics. This gives us an opportunity to learn from each other and to become more balanced within ourselves. However, we still struggle with the judgments that arise when our partner or family members are not acting in accordance with our wishes and would rather they display similar attributes and mannerisms like ourselves. If we could instead observe through the lens of curiosity, judgment would not supervene, and we may invite more wholeness into the entirety of the equation and into our lives.

When we deem one polarity, one way or one person as "better" than the other, with the added weight of judgment, separation is the result between the two, when all along they are really part of the same part and parcel.

Why limit ourselves when we could embrace the totality and entirety of both? Here is the opportunity to broaden the container and expand the parameters, where we can learn to become more accepting and patient with each other.

There has been a misconception in many arenas of life that we must focus on the light and only the light! That we must push back the darkness as it has no place here with us, lest it may taint and mar the purity of our virtuousness. Cultural and racial prejudices have given us full visibility on this matter in a humanity that has had a painstaking history toward the propensity of the judgment of opposites such as black and white, rich and poor.

When we stand in the sunlight, a shadow is cast, reminding us once again that they coexist in mutual tolerance despite their differences. The stronger the source of light, the darker a shadow is produced.

When we insist on focusing on the light as an exclusive path to "enlightenment," our shadow side will eventually be exposed and revealed. If we persistently push down into the depths of denial the parts of us we have deemed not good enough and unacceptable, this "shadow self" hides in the darkest corridors of our psyche and from our own self. As we focus more and more on the light, the light of consciousness will indeed shine right there in those hidden spots to bring them up and out to be seen and brought back into acceptance.

The more we deny the parts of ourselves that we are uncomfortable with—the unworthiness, the shame or guilt—the further down we push them, creating more density and heaviness in the body.

Eventually, our spirit becomes heavy, as well. This density creates an energetic block that can obstruct the light from shining into and through our body, which in turn casts more of a shadow.

As we insist on facing the light alone, we are limiting the capacity to heal into the wholeness of who we are. The hidden shadow needs to be embraced and accepted as part of the whole.

How do we welcome the shadow with the light?

The point of power is at the crux, at the fulcrum point between the two polarities. If we can stand at the center point without judgment and witness both sides as equally valid and divine as each other, we are at what I call the God Point. We can thus stand as masters of self, not being moved off-kilter to one side or the other. We can stand grounded between the two, riding the crest of the wave, standing at the fulcrum of the seesaw, in stillness and in freedom from this and that in the balance point. This is the yoga of living in the Union of the Divine.

One of my favorite quotes by Rowena Pattee Kryder in her book, *Sacred Ground to Sacred Space* is, "Dualities are opposite polarities of the same energetic force, which occur at the same pace to keep the universal energy in balance."

Even though light and shadow appear as separate entities, each defines the other to add definition to the structure of all things. One polarity cannot exist without the other as each has its perfect place in the totality of the greater design.

ACTIVATION

We are invited not to judge one aspect of polarity as better than the other, but to learn to feel and intuit the space that joins them, to observe their play not from the mind but from the heart, where the totality of a situation can be embraced in harmony and balance.

Sit quietly and watch how your thoughts may want to push and pull away from each other. Take a step back to stand at the fulcrum of your awareness to honor both as complements that can coexist and connect in greater harmony and union.

Merging the Opposing Forces of Duality into the Heart of Oneness

The American Oxford Dictionary defines duality as, "an instance of opposition or contrast between two concepts or two aspects of something; a dualism." Similarly, the Yin-Yang symbol of the Tao in ancient Chinese philosophy illustrates this perfect unison. The two teardrop shapes, one facing up and the other down, fit in opposite but perfect reflections of each other. One side, the color black, connotes the Yin, the more feminine and receptive principle; and the other side white, which connotes Yang, the masculine and more active principle. They each mirror their perfect opposite while each contains the essence of the other within it, depicted by the opposite color in a small dot within each. The Yin-Yang symbol represents harmony, unity and cooperation. They fit perfectly together, side by side, and yet each maintains its own significance and sovereignty.

We are constantly experiencing dual forces through the experience within our own bodies and that with the body of the Earth. Each inhale has its exhale, and each heartbeat has its opposites of contraction and expansion in its pulse. We have two brain hemispheres, each bringing equal and complementary contributions: one side linear and logical, the other lateral and creative. We ingest food in one end and excrete from the other.

On the longer wave pulse, we are delivered into this life alive through birth and depart through the passage of death. Within the larger template, our experience on Earth also clearly demonstrates this duality in perfect unison: through the momentum of Day and Night, Sun and Moon, Light and Shadow, North and South, Decay and Regeneration…to name a few.

These opposing forces of energy are in constant calibration to keep the universal balance and homeostasis in check. They are always moving with the tendency toward a relatively stable equilibrium between interdependent elements.

The body also has a primary goal: to maintain equilibrium in order to keep all systems and operations functioning at their peak optimum for proficient life and survival.

In constant flux within our lives, our state of mind, too, is contingent on this balance as we are faced with constant forces that pull us in opposite directions. The inner quarrel of, "Which is the 'right decision' to make? Can we trust the person in question or not?" and the economic, health and social decisions we are faced with keep us in constant flux. It can oftentimes feel like we are walking a tightrope. Walking a tightrope demands that we are maintaining our balance, treading the fine line in the middle of this way or that.

The duality of the mind is sustained by judgment, which causes separation. It is the judgments we make that tip us over from the balance of this fine line, right there between the dualities.

When we walk in balance, we are clear and sound in mind, confident in our stance and step. The moment we make a judgment, however, we have crossed the line and fallen into the trench of reaction, deeming one side more valid and divine than the other and "fallen out of grace," so to speak.

This constant play of opposites—of right and wrong, of better or worse—is playing havoc with our mental capacity to stay upright, sure and steady. This stress that stretches us from one side to the other is the tension on the weave of our fabric and psychological well-being, producing the constant rise and fall in our own perception of self. This leaves us feeling indecisive and in the shadow of doubt.

When we keep the whole equation in mind and heart—from the God Point of view—in truth, no one force of polarity is "more divine" or "more valid" than the other.

How, then, can we live and walk the line of balance between the two polarities?

We need to station our awareness at the fulcrum point of opposites, right at the center of the seesaw of our mind, centering ourselves in the still point where time and space have no place and the quiet and stillness of presence remains. We need to focus into the heart of existence: in the place that knows not of this or that, of me and them, or of past and future, but knows the way of the natural order or the balance of things, the harmony of the Yin-Yang, of the Tao.

At this site of witnessing, we are more able to observe and embrace both sides of any equation from the higher point of view. It is the witness self that I call the God Point of view (not the egoic self that creates separation through judgment by taking sides and making its own preference as to the right or better one). This is a continual practice in corralling our thoughts, training and focusing our mind to rest in peace in the still point between the two poles, into the heart of Oneness. I always proclaim, "Let us rest in peace while we are alive and well. Why wait until we die to rest in peace?"

Meditation is helpful to realize peace. It helps us sit in stillness and allow ourselves to *just be* right there with our body where presence can be felt. This can happen in just one moment...and then to the next moment and the moment after that. Just being simple and sitting with your body's presence without thinking; just *observing* without giving judgment to what you are sensing and feeling is helpful. It doesn't have to be called "meditation," it can be just sitting in stillness. Having the intention alone to drop from your head down into your body, into your heart and into what you are feeling without judgment is sufficient enough.

In this simplest act of stillness, we can take a deep inhale through the nose, followed by a long, slow exhale through the mouth. This allows for more of a *let go*, down into the body, into the nature of existence. From the head to the body, from the entangled mind to the ease of being, the breath ushers the electrical and static energy of our excessive thoughts and gives them somewhere to drop down into.

In the place of surrender, into the heart is where the presence of love awaits quietly and patiently. In this chamber of rest, thoughts and judgments cannot exist, but only love, in truth, remains.

At first, this practice may feel uncomfortable as we are now face to face with the shields we have placed over our hearts throughout the years. These shields guard and protect us to mitigate life's painful experiences of the past and/or fear of what is to come. As you continue to breathe into the "let go," you will begin to feel in between the inhale and exhale, in between each heartbeat and into the world of Oneness. Unity and Love awaits us here.

Even if it is only one moment that you feel this presence, this pure and most simple of spaces can reset and recalibrate your energy to a place of resolution and a higher resonance within. When you feel this calm space, just allow yourself to breathe into it, *let go* into it.

With practice, in time you will be able to speak from the presence of your body awareness and from your heart. For the body and heart know not of duality but embody unity with all life.

In this place, there is nothing to do and nowhere to go, but just be. In this place, you can listen in truth and trust in what your heart speaks of.

The heart needs to know that you are listening to it. It is usually the first thought, idea, or picture you receive before the mind comes into question or doubt what you hear or feel. The heart has no opposites, nor is it invested in duality as we know it. It is geared to unify, not separate; to love, not fear and hate; to understand, not judge; and to forgive the past into the present moment, into the presence of love.

ACTIVATION

When you are sitting quietly, allow your awareness to settle into the body. What is it feeling in this place right now? Can you allow the feeling to *just* be without judgment, or trying to change it in any way?

Let your heart know that you acknowledge its existence by listening to what it has to say. True listening comes from acknowledging what you hear without making it wrong or right.

You can now ask your heart questions that you can be present for, to listen to your inner truth without judgment and therefore without doubt. What does your inner self/heart need from you? What is the wisest route to take? How do you go about a situation that is bothering you?

Start to get to know your heart as a conscious part of your own being, as the place of higher counsel that will give you a non-biased and more holistic point of view from the Heart of Oneness.

Our Bio-Body-Computer

We are living bio-computers. Not from the manufacturers Apple, Dell, HP or Toshiba, but the Creator-Maker GD: God Direct.

We are not mere mechanical devices connected to a limited source of power, but biological, sentient beings who are connected to an unfathomable energy source that is beyond our scope of comprehension.

We contain an elaborate and extensive neural network, containing a galaxy of cells within a biosphere of life that continues to grow and evolve on its own merits. We have sensory faculties to hear, taste and smell, feel and see all the beauty before us; along with memory, instinct and intuition that enable us to sense beyond the physical senses. The body's ability to replicate, heal and regenerate our cells and the assimilation of nutrients all work in receptive and active flow toward the benefit of the whole.

This biological computer, our living body, doesn't have an external keyboard that we tap our fingers on to retrieve or access information on a screen. We do, however, have our own inner screen: our imagination and memory bank, which are archives of intelligence that we can tap into at any time.

The very instant we have a thought, it is like a finger tap on the "keyboard" that "downloads" this thought into a feeling and into an experience we can either use momentarily or archive for future use.

Each thought is the prime mover that instantaneously lights up our inner motherboard that activates this momentum.

Our bio-computers come with the latest operating system, generational upgrades, unlimited gigabytes and memory storage, along with our own inner recharging system. We are already super-multi-processing bio-computers of a superior kind. Humans have not yet acclaimed nor actualized the full capacity they each own and can access within themselves. We have taken this potentiality for granted, perhaps because it is given to us at no monetary cost.

Deeming this "mere" humanness as incidental, humanity, in our limited scope of what we have at our fingertips, seeks out to create mechanical devices to replace our own conceivable efficiency. We constantly seek the latest computer operating system that will give us access to more information, faster communication, or more distraction from self.

Our dependence on computers has enslaved us in the limited edition of self. We have come to rely on accessing information from a source of artificial intelligence at the expense of our own. Our brains have learned to calibrate with each tap of our fingers as we touch the keyboard and off we go, thrust into a world of illusion. We can ask a question and the answer is given. We search for ways to think, ways to go about a situation, what options we have at any given moment, and while this has become an invaluable tool, we have lost the real touch and pulse of the game. We have numbed our instinct and ability to tap into the deeper truth of who and what we are. This "touch and go" with each tap of the keyboard has dissipated our innate ability to "think and become," to access our superlative potential of our God-Direct apparatus.

Our advancement does not need to depend on an external mechanical device by tapping our fingertips to access "the all that maybe." Computers have exponentially helped evolve our world of communication as information is granted to us in all sectors of world affairs, news, fashion, health, how-to's and when-to's. But we can afford to pay more heed to what we can access and how we can access it within our own body/mind mechanisms. If we could rely less on external hardware devices and learn to sharpen and hone our inner adroitness and master senses, we have the capacity to experience something rather than just learn about it.

We are all interconnected by our thoughts that continue to create the world around us. Let us not divert and minimize the power of who and what we truly are, as creators of our reality. After all, we are told time and time again that we are created in the image of God.

ACTIVATION

Give recognition, credence and acceptance of the power and intelligence that lie within your own living bio-body-computer. Enjoy your computer and wonderful devices that can take you far and wide but never underestimate the ability you have in an instant to get an up-close and intimate, real, live version of yourself as well.

Getting Present,
Getting Embodied

If we look at the word "present" and break it up phonetically, we see "pre-sent." The Present brings forth each moment that is pre-sent to us from beyond time and space, appearing to us with pre-born innocence that is intact and untainted from the past and of the future. It presents to us a new opportunity to start again, to start afresh.

The Present is a gift from the Divine that keeps on giving, reminding us to open to new and all possibilities. It affords us the opportunity to start again in each and every moment. Being present allows us to drop the heavy baggage and burden we carry of the past and also spares us from frantically running our minds loose into the worry of the future. We can allow life to be less encumbered, easier, and lighter.

The same can be said of the word "presence," as in "pre-sense." It is the state we can tap into prior to the use of our physical senses. We are perpetually immersed in presence, this natural state of primeval and innate intuition. It is the original beingness of pure intact reception that we could call the state of Grace.

This pre-sent, pre-sense energy moves through us endlessly. It is ever abundant. It is not of a limited supply, or only available to the few. It has no judgment and no agenda other than to be pre-sent from the Divine. It is not dependent on whether we are aware of it or not; however, if you are aware of its presence, then it is made known to you.

Consciousness happens, but are you aware of being conscious? This presence affords us new life, new opportunities to reinvent ourselves and recreate our lives in each transpiring moment.

Children help us to remember that this is possible: to live life to its fullest and to receive life's moments as they arise. They are not yet fully adulterated with the program of analysis of the hows and whys and why-nots. They are instead more open to the magic of life as it unfolds in each moment. In such presence, their innocence keeps them close to the Divine, to their original sentience.

In the book *Way of the Peaceful Warrior*, Dan Millman says, "When you lose your mind, you come to your senses." In other words, when we get out of the way, we can sense more into our body and start living a fuller experiential life without tainting it with too much thought and judgment. It is about living and experiencing our lives through the body; through the *feeling* of it rather than the idea or concept of it. This is what we may refer to as pure embodiment. In other words, we can understand and respect that we are of Spirit; a field of energy; of a Life Force that is made manifest in the physical.

Everything we feel is registered in our body; our bio-computer. The body never lies; it is an expression of Divine Truth and is actually innocent in each moment, expressing and reflecting to us how we actually feel. The mind can complain, whinge and moan and lie, but the body never lies, giving us a reality check on our own living hourglass of where we are "really at."

We are a repository of all that we have come to be; a bio-computer that holds the records of our ancestry, our soul incarnations, our spirit force, and the synthesis of all our personified experiences. Our physical bodies are the vehicles with which we travel through this collective field of present-time energy as we move through our life's journey.

Our soul gleans and harnesses wisdom through pure experience alone rather than from what happens to us in circumstance. Not from the external reality of our relationships, our career, a divorce, or our creative endeavors, but from how we register the *feelings* of what we do, of what stirs the greater emotion, passion, and compassion within us. When we take our final breath in life, it is not the career or how much money we have or about anybody else that counts. Your soul will register the experience you have mustered and more importantly, how you truly feel about yourself. It is the inner self-enrichment we accrue that affords us the understanding, the knowledge, and finally the wisdom of self.

If we could bring more awareness to the body of our experience by stepping into the purity of the pre-sent and pre-sense in each moment, we could lighten up the load of guilt, shame, and emotions that can rob us of our original innocence.

As we practice becoming more cognizant of our body—of the entirety of who we have become until this present moment—we become more available to what life is showing us. We can then truly experience the fullness of life and be more connected with our feelings that ultimately become the registry of our soul.

How else can we feel the awareness of presence but through the body?

In the sessions with my clients, I first look to see what the body is expressing in the present moment. I trust this as a measure of where to navigate the session rather than rely on what my client is conveying through spoken words. Of course, I carefully listen to every word they speak as they need to express and communicate their story, their experience is valid, but more credence is given to what the *body* is suggesting. I look at their bodily movements and the tension in the areas of their body in which they hold that emotion.

The body speaks in the language of truth. It is a wordless language: their hands convey in action what is really going on, beyond what the mind insists on saying to the outside world; the tone of voice, how hard the jaw is held while speaking, or their foot may be stiff while the rest of their face has a smile placed over the torment of anguish and pain.

Once again, the body never lies. When we see someone walking with their shoulders hunched over, we sense a feeling of defeat as they walk their path in a somewhat less-confident manner. When we see someone walking with their shoulders back and upright, we sense more confidence and positivity. No matter what we try to hide—whether it is our racked-up thoughts or the entanglements in our mind—the body, in its commitment to presence, reveals the truth in each moment.

How can we anchor this amorphous energy, this living presence in our body?

Through the conscious use of Breath. The breath is what connects us to this living pre-sent energy, known as chi or prana. In the ancient Hawaiian culture, it is known as mana. We can exercise conscious breathing to connect us to this living energy and power.

Breathe into the parts of you that have become frozen with fear and forgotten in time; the parts of you that you have deemed "less than." There may be parts of you that are screaming for your attention with sensations of tension and pain. It is in those moments of fear, fright, and trauma where you stopped breathing and locked the fear into the muscles that become stored as muscle memory, which warps and contorts the body from its uniform state.

When we breathe, we are ALIVE. Whether it be a positive or negative feeling, we experience life in its fullness. But when we hold our breath and stop breathing, we deaden the feelings we don't want to feel. Each time we do that, we are taking one step closer to the finish line—the "deadline"—of our life.

Presence is here to give you a new moment of relinquishment, to renounce your past. The breath is how we can wash away our fears and our tears. Presence whispers to us that all is well in this present moment and the next and the next. The mystic Osho, also known as Rajneesh, in his discourses would ask, "Is there a problem in this moment?" I remember asking myself this very question at a most critical moment in my life when I felt stuck and with the feeling that there was nowhere to go and no one to help. I was washing my hands and asked this question to myself, "Amalia, is there a problem in this moment?" I found myself answering from that moment that replied, "NO, there is never a problem in this moment as there is no past attached to complain about or a fear of an unknown future that exists here. The point of power is in the present moment!"

It was at that point when I came to realize that it is being in the moment that resurrects you back into life, into the quiet of Grace, of the pre-sent and the pre-sense to start again anew. I had never washed my hands with so much presence and aliveness as I had then.

ACTIVATION

Take a few breaths into the spaces of your body that feel tense. Be present with the tension as it is, without a preference of how you would rather it be. Let it be seen and felt, as that is all that is required, for it is in acceptance that presence resides.

The pre-sent moment will release the tension and forgive the past. An easy practice in being in the moment is to stay present while eating and drinking. Try not to think or worry while you are chewing your food. Enjoy the fullness of your life experience with every mouthful. Make this a daily practice to hone your skill in experiencing each moment with the presence of your living embodiment.

Rising to the Occasion of
Our Sovereign Self

Each and every one of us throughout the generations holds a blueprint within our DNA for the coming age we are entering into. We come fully equipped, body, mind and soul, able and ready! The newer generations especially come in with neural knowledge at their fingertips for computer and technological sciences that evolve at such a high speed. They are cable ready!

Our soul's journey, from light-years beyond time and space, provides us with all that we need to deal with our trials and tribulations in order to assist in our Greater Becoming. We are Denizens of Light that have chosen to descend from Spirit into Matter—into a body—to assist in making the quantum leap from the edge of humanity into the New Earth Community we are preparing for.

We come into these bodies with all the physical, emotional and mental attributes we need for the tests that our souls need us to pass through, for our higher degree of learning. Within this journey of trial and initiation, we can fall prey to the talons of the predatory powers of division, denial, and controlling systems that exercise control over the state of our affairs. The general populace has submitted to this fallacy of a distorted and fabricated power that overrides them, clipping their wings from their own inherent freedom. Our independence and liberation are at stake. The time and age have come to reclaim our power as sole proprietors to our internal truth and to our *soul proprietorship* of our higher truth. It is time to take our personal lives to the next level and revolutionize our humanity into an integrated species of unity, collaboration, co-operation and co-creation.

The hippies of the 60s, known as the Flower Children, were ridiculed for their idealistic movement toward a new-age paradigm of love, peace and freedom. They seeded the co-operative, co-creative, collaborative living with a common purpose of unity, in harmony and abidance with the land, planting organic free-of-pesticide gardens. They were guardians of Earth who fought for green energy, recycling of plastics, saving the oceans and clearing pollution, working toward free energy systems. They were the collective that practiced non-judgment, rearing their children to strive toward love and peace, not war. They knew of the covert power of the oppressive thumb and fought to reclaim ownership of their sovereignty, to restore the balance.

It has only been in the last few decades or so that the fabric of our society has begun to anchor these sustainable practices that the Flower Children were fighting for: to care for our planet and the generations to come. Like the Flower Children, the indigenous peoples of the Earth Work with the Seventh Generation Principle, which is based on the creed that every decision made today should result in a sustainable world seven generations into the future. The decisions made about the integrity of our water, our natural resources and the health industry must ensure the propagation of life for future generations. These decisions are not made at the expense of our children, but rather to pay it forward to them. We must start thinking of the Earth we are leaving our children and children's children. It is time to rise to the occasion and stand in our sovereign selves to pay our unsettled dues and ensure we can meet the imminent change on our planet for a better outcome for future generations. It is in the palm of our hands as New Earth is rising. The time is Now.

Let us expand beyond the limitations into the fullness of who and what we are. As Denizens of Light, we have traveled a long way from soul to body, and from body to soul we shall return again. We are on a collective journey of remembrance, where we are endowed with all we need within our very make-up to rise to the occasion, reclaim our power and restore our sovereignty.

ACTIVATION

Look within yourself and in your relationships to see where you have given your power away. It starts right there with you. Have you bent too far and lost your upright stance? Make an internal inventory to check what attributes you have come in with, the inner gifts and qualities that you have, and how they could affect a better world around you.

Diving into the
Void of All-Oneness

At all costs, most of us distract ourselves to avoid the deep emptiness and loneliness we hide under the mask of popularity and self-sufficiency. We are unfamiliar with our aloneness and confuse it with being our "poor little lonely self." Our aloneness is not run by fear or the drive to reach out to something or someone to fill the sense of emptiness and lonesomeness we may feel. It does not distract us from the discomfort when we are on our own. Aloneness is a place within us that grants us space to feel, to contemplate and to wonder. It is the space within that when relaxed into, connects us with the greater feeling of Oneness.

The truth is that each and every one of us is alone. As souls, each one of us enters the world alone and leaves the world alone. We don't take our partners, our children, our possessions or our professions with us. However, what we do take with us is our repository of feelings, experiences, and lessons that we have gleaned throughout our lives.

Each of us harnesses this life experience on our own. Yes, we do have the help of others, but we are ultimately alone in our individual life-soul journey. It is vital and life-soul preserving to be comfortable in our aloneness, in the space of time, in the privacy of our own self, to reflect, build upon and be comfortable with our self in order to build the bank of wisdom we carry to the other side.

Many of us learned what "lonely" felt like when we sought out solace from the intensity of our family dynamics, to find a place of peace and quiet. We needed somewhere where we could "soothe and heal our wounds," hold our dolls or play with our toy trucks to ensure we were feeling safe in unsound situations. We may very well associate being "alone" with such childhood experiences that trigger the discomfort, which drives us to distraction or to seek out someone to "make it feel better." To feel alone is to feel that there is no one around to ease this discomfort; however, all too often, many who are in relationships or even large families still feel alone even though they are in constant contact with the other.

It is valuable to distinguish the difference between loneliness and our aloneness. In our loneliness we are in the feeling of isolation of separateness from others; and in our aloneness, we feel connected to the greater whole and supported at all times, whether we are in the company of others or not.

If we break up the word "aloneness," we can come to "all-oneness." In our aloneness—our *All-Oneness*—we are not alone but supported by the universe, the unseen elements within the force of nature, the angels, our guides and guardians and ancestors. We feel the connection in the web of life and know that we are an integral part of the whole.

Discovering Aloneness:

I first discovered this aloneness at the bottom of the ocean at the age of eight. My Greek family with its countless members—aunts and uncles, cousins and friends—would go on regular picnics to the country and to the ocean. On one of these momentous of days, we were at the beach where my assorted cousins were splashing and laughing in the waters and the Greeks were conversing, eating and dancing in merriment. The way they communicated with each other often sounded like they were arguing and shouting at each other, perhaps because they needed to increase the volume of their voices for each to be heard in such a large group and to override the blaring Greek music.

It seemed that I was always a little different in terms of my depth of feeling and understanding of things, and there I was again, setting myself apart to delve into the greater expanse beyond what was expected and accepted. As my Greek family shouted and hooted and my cousins splashed each other in the water, I wondered what the ocean was feeling in all of this. Did it have its own awareness of its existence? I had a notion that if I sunk to the bottom of the ocean, that I could sense into what it may be feeling. I could just lie there as if I wasn't even there myself, to see what it would be like to become the ocean and to disappear into nothingness. It wasn't that I had a desire to see what death might feel like, but rather a dissolution into the ocean itself, into the greater mystery of what I did not understand. I asked myself, "What is the ocean feeling and thinking? What type of personality does it have?" I could sense a current of energy uniting the vast body of water and wanted to know more.

I took a deep breath, held onto my nose and tried to sink my body down. I soon realized that I needed to exhale so that I would not float up again, so I expunged the breath from my body and tried once more. I sank to the bottom of the ocean where I met a quiet, dark, velvety and restful silence. I could no longer hear the cacophony of noise from my demonstrative family. It was there where I could rest in peace, where I learned how it may feel to die; to not be here; to disappear into complete nothingness, into the Void.

The strange thing was that although I felt a nothingness, there was a feeling of completion; a sense that everything, that all possibilities could exist at the same time.

The ocean taught me to not be afraid of being alone; how not to be afraid of the unknown and of death. It showed me how to rest in my aloneness. Yes, I was alone in the dark of the ocean, but in my aloneness I felt embraced in the all-encompassing and restful nothingness, in the Void at the bottom of Self, at the deepest part of my being. The Void is a place that can reveal the disappearance and appearance of nothingness and everythingness, of finish and start, a place to reset and begin anew.

Little did my family ever know what I was truly getting up to or into. The shamanic way has always walked by my side.

A Shamanic Practice:
The Well of Being:

In my shamanic healing practice, when a client reveals a hidden and deep sense of terror of being "alone," I guide them through a process to embrace this fear in a safe and gentle way in order to meet with the Void within.

Allow me to take you along this journey.

Begin by taking three deep breaths, in through the nose and out through the mouth. Allow the body to drop into its physicality and with each exhale, let go. On the third exhale, follow the breath as if you *are* the breath and feel it roll all the way down to the base of your spine, in the root chakra area where the buttocks rests on where you are sitting. Surrender each breath as you exhale through this root chakra area and let it flow into Mother Earth to ground your energy. When you are settled in this place, take a few breaths to feel the safety and security that this place within you can bring.

Now imagine that you are at the top of a deep well and that you are looking down into it. Hold a large rock in your hands and drop it into the opening of the well. Once you have let it go, follow the rock down. Become the rock sinking deeper and deeper down into the well, into the darkness, into the depths. Keep following the rock down until it reaches and lands at the bottom of the well, where it can go no more. Let yourself be the rock at the bottom of the well.

What are you feeling at the bottom of the well? Do you feel cold, dark and alone? Or do you feel silent, peaceful and restful? Either way is exactly right for you. This is not an exercise in judgment or comparison, it is an opportunity to embrace the feelings as they arise in the moment.

If you feel the coldness, the darkness and the loneliness at the bottom of the well, breathe into the feelings, in through the nose and out of the mouth. Just let the feelings be felt without judgment, without wanting to change them or escape and avoid them. Once felt "as it is" without reaction, it is as if you are shining light on the darkness and fear can no longer exist in that moment.

Or if you are feeling peaceful and restful in your aloneness at the bottom of the well, breathe into it. Let yourself feel the ease, the stillness and quiet. Let your body register it and allow the nervous system to be informed that you can be comfortable in your aloneness, that you can rest in peace while you are alive and not buy into the belief that you can only rest in peace once you die. Figuratively speaking, it is the ego mind that has to die in order to feel the peace within. It is the imbalanced ego mind that fights the aloneness and insists you are lonely and therefore need to seek out the distraction to fill the void within.

Just like the rock that is dropped over the edge of the well, we are invited to let go from the edge of restraint into the pool of the unknown. It feels scary to do such an ungodly thing, to dive deeper into that place of yourself that is unfamiliar; into the Void of Self; into the vacuity of your mind; into the open space of self, where you are alone in the All-Oneness.

The Void is called by different names in varied arenas. Scientists and astronomers know it as the black hole, where nothing exists but the vacuum. To meteorologists it is known as the eye of the hurricane storm, where the watchful eye is held still at the center of the spin that surrounds it. In psychiatry it is referred to as the void of hopelessness and depression, and in the Goddess traditions it is known as the Womb of Creation from which the birth of life arises and comes to pass.

The Void is mostly associated, however, with the black hole that can consume and devour us; a place that we could be lost in forever; a place of loneliness and desolation. But the Void within us is not a black hole that steals our living force. It is the deep well of stillness and the silence of conscious space; a place of pure potential, of pure energy waiting to be inspired into action.

It is a holy place where we can actually rest in the absence of distraction of the doing mind. The ego mind easily and willingly interprets it as a death sentence of its very own self, for the ego mind cannot exist in this deep well of presence. We in the Western world in particular have unresolved fear around death and will do whatever it takes to avoid it so long as we shall live. Instead, we try to fill the hole—the Void within—by constantly reaching out for something, or grappling for others to fill the empty space we resist when we feel alone.

As we spend more time getting to know the Void within, we can become more aware and understand the nature of it. Instead of relating to it as an intimidating and threatening force, we could remain calm and curious about it, feel it and fill it with the light of our own consciousness. Like the rock that sinks to the bottom of the well, we too can drop down into our deeper knowingness and let ourselves sink into the depth of our well-being. The restful place of no-thing-ness is where we can rest in peace, and touch into the potential possibilities of the all-thing-ness, from the shamanic death place to a place of rebirth.

The Void of the Universe:

After my first experience of the Void at the bottom of the ocean, my next encounter with it was in my sleep after a rather unusual experience at school at the age of twelve.

There had been a couple of young teachers, a man and a woman, who led us through a rather curious meditation/visualization. They asked us to lie on our backs and took us through a relaxation of the body. They then asked us to visualize lifting up out of our bodies, then above the ceiling, rising higher above to see our school, then our town, then our state, then higher and higher to see our country and then our planet… It was thrilling to experience this kind of perspective. To have such a broad view way beyond our small little school and town. It seemed harmless enough and I felt I was a natural at this kind of exploration, so I thought I would give it a go on my own that night as I drifted off to sleep.

At first, I lifted off my bed and could see myself floating just above the ceiling of my bedroom. Then I followed the instructions just as the teachers directed and allowed myself to lift even further above my house, then up into the night sky, to see my town, then my state, then my country of Australia and then out into the dark sky with the stars and planets. I seemed to have traveled far and wide and was comfortable doing so until... *Uh oh!*

I had come to a pitch-blackness of what looked like the edge of the Universe. It had a consciousness to it that felt foreboding, unfathomable; it did not feel too welcoming, it seemed to convey that it was not a place for me and that if I approached any further I may not ever return. Terrified and with not a moment of hesitation, I retracted back to my bed in a flash!

Back in my bed is where I wanted to be. It didn't feel lonely but rather more of an existential aloneness, that we are all alone. That planet Earth is alone even though it is teeming with life and inhabitants.

I knew that I could not explain to anybody at the time what I had seen and felt, both at the bottom of the ocean and at the edge of the Universe. I felt that this subject was taboo and out of limits, so I dropped the inquiry and did not let myself go into anything that may have felt or looked like "the Void" for a very long time until...decades later!

In the Blackness of the Great Pyramid of Cheops:

My third major encounter with the Void was at the age of twenty-eight in the Great Pyramid of Cheops, during a rebirthing intensive retreat in Egypt with Sondra Ray, Bob and Mallie Mandel and Fredric Lehrman, some of the greats at the time who were spreading the teachings about consciousness and breathwork back in the 80s.

We had paid baksheesh, which was a kind of bribe to the gate-keeper, to let us enter the Great Pyramid of Cheops and into the King's Chamber one early morning well before the hordes of tourists were due to arrive. We had the guards turn off the lights so we could experience the energy of the pyramid without being distracted by our visual senses.

I was startled when the lights went out. It was pitch black! My eyes were wide open but there was not one sign of light, shadow, or movement to be seen. There was nothing but dense, blinding black-ness; not-a-thing to show a reference point outside of myself and I felt as if I might dissolve into nothingness and everythingness at the same time.

I felt completely untethered from everything, as there was no point outside of myself in which to orient my mind. *This is the Void,* I thought, in a state of ever-increasing awe. *The unfathomable place where the known and unknown meet, where love and fear dance together in perfect step and counterstep, where the light and dark converge.*

In the darkness Absolute, the energy had reached a pitch and with no frame of reference, I suddenly felt birthed into a new state of awareness, as if my eyes opened wide to the blind eye of creation. I was not afraid!

It was there in the ancient chamber deep within the earth that the Void revealed itself to me again. I saw where the eye of the hur-ricane storm began its journey toward the light, where the origin of energy within the dark Womb of Creation sows its seeds of life.

In the deep space of every atom's center, too, is where the black hole—the Void—lies. It rests at the center of Creation, where the mystery of pure potentiality exists. The Void of Consciousness is there to be met, and it is up to us to become familiar with it and to co-create with it; to bring consciousness into unconsciousness and light into the dark. Moving into the frontiers of the unknown is part of our evolution that drives and guides the borders of our success.

No, the Void within is not a place to be afraid of. If we truly let go and surrender the ego into the still center of self—into the deeper space of silence within us—we will be granted a place of clear-seeing light. Once we face our greatest fear of being alone, of death and of the unknown, we can sink down into the bottom of our well-being and rest in peace, into the place of our origin, into the pulsating potentiality of life from which we arose.

ACTIVATION

Allow some time to sink into and sit in the depth of silence with the still point of Creation. Relax into the dark spaces between the thoughts of the mind. Settle down into it and rest in the peace that resides there.

Practice this in your quiet time or meditation to become familiar with this place within you. This will help you connect to the greater whole of existence. Here you will find you are not lonely and in fear of this seeming separation, but instead, you will be able to tap into the aloneness...the All-Oneness.

Operation Sting

A sting operation is a tool used by local, state, federal and international agencies to resolve illegal acts. A typical sting will have a law enforcement officer or cooperative member of the public play a role as a criminal partner or potential victim who goes along with a suspect's actions to gather evidence of the suspect's wrongdoing. In doing so, they put a stop to the "wrongdoing" and bring "justice and right action" to the situation.

We experience this type of scenario in our lives on a continuous basis, where our Higher Self acts as the law-abiding officer to seek out the "culprit"—the part of our ego that contrives and conspires to keep us hostage to our lower self; to our lower self-esteem—to the part of ourselves that believes it is not or never good enough, that thinks we will never amount to anything, that we are alone, that we are unlovable, unacceptable, unattractive, and that we are inherently a failure to some degree or another.

This lower self has us believe that we "are all of that" and not much more. As a result, it starts to behave like a fugitive in our own life, no matter how law-abiding we may be. As a result, we unconsciously designate, magnetize and appoint other role players with the perfect physical attraction, magnetism of chemistry and attributes that dovetail with our beliefs. We then play and live out the "not good enough" notion or any other scheme of sorts, designating accomplices to enact this setup along the way.

It is our Higher Self that ultimately "sets up" this sting operation, to coax out the perpetrator: the ego. On the contrary, the healthy Ego's original purpose is to protect us from being hurt or from feeling pain, and enables us to set up healthy boundaries so that we can live a healthy, functional and safe life. The unsolicited ego, however, effectively becomes the perpetrator: the deceptive member that can keep us hostage to these patterns.

Universal Truth always has its sight on a correct path for us and sets up this "heist" to eventually coax out the perpetrator. This is set in place so we can flush out the pain and suffering, the madness and untruth that you are unworthy or that you are unlovable and unacceptable. This reenactment is played out again and again until the perpetrator—the ego—is nabbed and the fugitive within you that is running and hiding from the law and light of Truth is arrested.

You see, wherever there is a falsity, there is the truth. The truth that sits on the other end of the seesaw in the equal and opposite polarity is the Law of Universal Balance.

The Law of abiding Truth waits for the right time and steps in for Operation Sting to arrest the unsolicited ego, which has well strayed from its original cause: to protect us.

The higher ordinance of our Higher Self operates in perfect unison to bring us to higher ground, to love the seemingly unlovable within ourselves, to raise our consciousness toward the wholeness of "the truth and nothing but the truth" that each of us are. With its love, it shines the light on this lower self that has been hiding in the shadows of terror like a running fugitive. In this Light, it can no longer hide, nor run, and has to take the stand in front of the greater Law of Truth.

We have come to identify ourselves with this lower hiding self and do not realize that Love in Truth will bring justice to any situation. We often feel victimized and held hostage in these scenarios that keep reappearing in our lives over and over again, and fight this greater Law of Manifestation as if it is the one that is working against us. But it is instead the higher force that enters our sting operation to bring this type of delinquency into right action. It is for our highest good, for our better growth, so that we can evolve into more of who we can truly be *and are.*

ACTIVATION

Ask your Higher Self to bring in the higher force of light to shine on your lower self in order to bust the operation sting of your unsolicited ego.

Be gentle in your manner of exposing it to the light by bringing love to the situation as you coax it out of hiding.

Allow the understanding that the Light of Truth will discharge the hidden shadow, and in place bring the justice of Love to yourself and your life.

Karma vs. Destiny

Many of us have heard of the word "karma" before as it has become a hip word most likely incorporated in a movie, a song, in spiritual studies or in a horoscope reading. We may have a general idea of what is and how it is said to affect us. According to the New Oxford American Dictionary, karma means (in Hinduism and Buddhism), "the sum of a person's actions in this and previous states of existence, viewed as deciding their fate in future existences."

A more encompassing way of looking at karma is the cause-and-effect dynamic, where the seeds we sow today are the fruits we will harvest tomorrow. If we sow an apple seed, an apple tree will grow. If we plant an unkind seed in our mind, we will surely reap an uncharitable or unsympathetic outcome.

Our actions create repercussions of consequences that occur some time after our actions. A re-percussion is to strike or impact a situation that can create an echo or reverberation effect. For everything has an equal and opposite polarity in order to keep the universal balance in check. This lies in the parameter of the Law of the Universe, the Law of Action and Reaction that dances between the dualities within ourselves and in our lives that holds us accountable for our actions.

We are ever perplexed as to what karma truly is, and how and why it affects us. Quite flippantly, we blame karma for things that "happen to us," saying "that's karma for you," or "karma is a bitch," forgetting that we are each the seed planters and the harvesters of the fruit of those seeds we ourselves planted.

All too often, we get lost in the details of our lives that illustrate the same patterns and outcomes, no matter how much we try to change the storyline. We try every trick in the book to change the circumstances, to affect a more preferable outcome in our lives. We aim to be nicer, attempt the opposite approach to situations, deaden and nullify our senses with food, medications, drugs, and more often point the finger at others rather than turning it toward ourselves. Yet we usually end up with the same feelings of loss, disappointment and unworthiness, feeling unsupported and hopeless around the patterns that continue to ensue.

In the Western world in particular, we have been given a limited definition of and are entrained to think about karma in a more retributive stance that keeps us in the role of victim. It has kept us unsuspecting of the true power we may hold.

We have missed the mark! It is not the storyline that bounces us back and forward into this rebounding effect, but our beliefs and feelings about ourselves that need to be brought back in line. The seeds that are planted in the soil of our own consciousness need to be examined, for if we plant into the field of our mind negatory and bitter thoughts, then we surely cannot expect to reap sweet, juicy fruit as a result. From the book *A Course in Miracles*: "There is no point in trying to change the world. It is incapable of change because it is merely an effect. But there is indeed a point in changing your thoughts about the world. Here you are changing the cause. The effect will change automatically."

The most effective way to handle karma is to lean into the present-now-moment. The past has evaporated into the recesses of history and the future is a fantasy yet to come. Scientists are now admitting that the past, present and future all exist in the moment of now. That Time as we know it does not actually exist in truth.

So how could karma affect us if we live in the clear slate of the present moment? Presence in consciousness is not governed by time and therefore cannot concede to judgment, that only arises from an attachment to the past or future. Easy enough to say, but let us take a look at a way we can each practice to be more effective with the actions we choose to take.

When we experience our feelings, it is important to feel them as they arise without dragging the long-haul of the past into it and asking why this happened to us. Asking yourself why this pattern keeps arising to gain clear insight and understanding is one thing, but continuously asking from the "victim" place of blame and shame can hold us hostage in the loop of torment. This shift requires taking full responsibility for the outcomes in our lives as a perfect reflection of the thoughts and beliefs that we continue to broadcast to the outside world.

Becoming accountable for your own self-made reality is your sole business. It is your "soul proprietorship" that only you can take care of and manage. It is, therefore, nobody else's business, hence there is no one "out there" to blame and point the finger toward.

When those recurring "outcomes" of being betrayed, feeling invalidated, taken advantage of, money slipping through your fingers or attracting the same abuse from others makes you feel like you are circling through a revolving door—stop!

Take inventory and ask yourself, "What is under this rock I have been hesitant to lift? What is behind this mask, this false face that I hide behind? What lies under the surface of self that is asking to be met, to be accepted and loved in the present moment?"

Instead of asking *why* this is happening, which keeps you in the same loop scenario, ask yourself, "What can I do to make a rightful change? What must I be thinking to create this loop? How can I practice benevolent and loving thoughts about myself in order to create a different outcome?" It is time to stop running from the power within and turn your sight inward for the answers you seek!

Behind the mask and under the rock lie the hidden things and feelings about ourselves that we alone have invalidated and judged. We can affect a positive outcome by looking at the income of our own values and our own self-worth. As we release the past in the present, we liberate our future!

It can be very challenging to turn our sight and awareness inward to "sense into our feelings," to get out of the mind of past and future, and to get into our bodies and truly listen to our feelings in the present moment. (See "Presence as the Art of Being: How Can We Deal with Pain.")

Our thoughts can keep us hostage to the fraudulence of self as they tend to lie and hustle their way to the frontline of pretense. It can be challenging to maintain equanimity by listening to the deeper sensation of our feeling-body. But the body never lies; it is a pure reflection of what we are thinking, believing and feeling, just as our lives are a pure reflection of our thoughts and beliefs about ourselves.

More concerned with the outer world than the inner world, we have strayed from our inner compass point, our True North, so to speak. We have lost ourselves in the story and are walking in circles on the treadmill of the karmic loop. We have forgotten the inner guide who is in authorship of navigating our path along the way.

Does karma lead us to our destiny?

We are just as familiar with the word "destiny" as we are with karma. Many of us were raised with the storybook mythos where the hero or heroine was led along the path of their destiny to save a princess or a village. The storybook character was either born into fame or famine, or luck or lack of fortune would predetermine their providence. According to Merriam-Webster's dictionary, "destiny" means "a predetermined course of events often held to be an irresistible power or agency."

If karma is the seed of which you sow, then destiny is the fruit that you reap. If karma is the arrow of the past that is pulled back and aimed in a certain direction, then destiny is where the arrow thrusts into the time and space of our future. They are both each other's counterparts; the two cannot exist without each other as they move in sync around the compass point of the thoughts and beliefs we carry out in our lives.

If Karma is in the south, then Destiny's arrow is pointing north! Each direction is balanced by the other in perfect union. When we move off the either/or points of the compass and choose to stand at the center of the dial instead, standing in the present between either direction of past and future, then we are not at the effect of either course. We can be present to the situation, to make more clear and present choices that are not arising out of the fear of the past and the anticipation of the future.

Standing in the presence of mind and body allows us to stand back and witness the situation as it is, beyond the monkey mind that cannot be trusted to tell you the truth. It is in the present moment from which the compass point leads us to our Providence, (Provide-ence) beyond cause and effect, beyond karma as we have known it to be.

As we begin to stand in our center and feel our feelings without judgment in our given moments, we can stand in the most powerful posture of the Universe. It is this place where we begin to create new beginnings in a more untainted way. We can create from a place of freedom, from a place where our story is not attached to the karmic effect of cause and effect, of action and reaction, but from a place of our original innocence between the two polarities. If we can practice standing in this point of presence, we may not be subject to this loop of polarity. Herein lies our freedom from the wheel of Karma and Destiny.

ACTIVATION

What are the thoughts you spin around the wheel of karma in your own mind of creation? Check to see what seed of origin your thoughts sow. Look deeply in the soil of your consciousness to neutralize and equalize your thoughts. Allow for the innocence of being to flourish.

The Greater Bird Tribe:
Angels and Pigeons

Many of us make a habit of deeming which feathers of a bird hold more significance and value. Whether they be of the eagle, the hawk, the owl, the finch, the sparrow, the flicker bird or the pigeon, each and every feather holds high value. For they are all of the winged tribe, messengers of Spirit that teach us about flight, balance and observing our lives from a higher perspective.

Angels, too, are part of the greater winged tribe, as they take flight back and forth from Heaven to Earth as messengers of Spirit. They descend from the heavenly realms to awaken the sleeping masses in a world that knows of pain, suffering, calamity and separation. Their wings, broad and wide, embrace mercy and forgiveness without judgment of this or that, of you or I, or of good or bad; but instead enfold into their wings of love, the humanness with all of its errings and stirrings.

As human angels, we have also descended from our soul-spirit place into the material plane and into a physical body to take steps in understanding the human plight. We, in our aspiration toward the expansion of freedom, are here to learn how to spread our wings wide open, to take flight in our breadth of vision and imagination.

We hold in the banks of our memory the truth of who we are in the I Am Presence. We have come to learn how to love ourselves and to love our brothers and sisters of humanity, for in our hearts lie a storehouse of love, compassion and forgiveness.

Our shoulder blades, the very remnants of our angel wings, are living proof that we are also angels who had to forfeit our wings in order to walk and stay connected to the material plane. Our two arms extend from our hearts to express the love that we entrust to the world. The right and left wings are the two sides of the scales that exemplify balance and righteous posture. We cannot soar in flight of the Spirit World with only one wing; with only one-sided seeing. One-sided seeing engenders judgment and separation that weighs us down and plummets us to the ground.

At the end of our lifespans, we "lift off" in our ascent heaven-wards through the winds of change, back through the veils of illusion and just like Pigeons, we make the return flight as couriers of Spirit to deliver our message and wisdom back to home base...to soul place. Metaphorically speaking, our voyage here in this world begins with descending as Angels from Heaven and ascending as Pigeons from Earth to courier our messages and experiences from our earthly incarnation back home to Source.

In this way, we make our descent into the physical before we make our ascent back to Spirit-Source. We land on the ground with light and love that we have brought with us from the heavenly realms as it continues to shine through and from us. We are here to ground this light into the darkest and densest of planes, into unconsciousness, into the density as true Angels would. We are here to watch out for and heal the separation with love, to anchor the new vision with light, to be a messenger of Spirit to heal humanity. We intrinsically know we are to make our flight passage back to God-Source, Father-Mother God, and as homing Pigeons we know exactly how to get there...to our home place.

The Ancient Egyptians held great knowledge and usage of the bird tribes as seen on hieroglyphs, from the falcon to the vulture, depicting either their descent into the Underworld or their flight through this world to the next during the passage of death and rebirth.

As both Angels and Pigeons, we could very well call ourselves "Angeons" as we make our descent and ascent to the lower and upper worlds. Either bird is no more sacred than the other; one feather is no more significant than the other; one of us is no more worthy of the other. For as part of the greater bird tribe—the winged ones—we are each flight bearers, messengers and couriers of Spirit.

ACTIVATION

The next time you see a feather, no matter what bird it belongs to, honor it as part of the greater winged tribe of which you are a part of. Hold it in high regard as a spiritual totem that may represent your greater passage through the worlds of known and unknown, of death and rebirth, as an Angel and a Pigeon...as an Angeon.

Religion vs. Spirituality

Our belief systems often act as scaffolding that supports the toppling towers of our mind. Scaffolding is brought into place as a temporary structure when a building is either being restored or needs support to stand erect. Religion, as it stands today, is the very scaffolding that supports the crumbling framework of man's inner faith. With the complex interconnected systems of information technology, governmental institutions, economy, education, bureaucracy, and entertainment, man is indeed in need of a restorative faith.

There are thousands of religions worldwide, churches, denominations, religious bodies, faith groups, tribes, cultures, and movements, each distinguished by the differentiation of culture, customs, and creeds. Each calls "their" God by a different name. From Allah, Brahma, Shiva, Amun-Ra, Jehovah, Yahweh, Wakan Tanka—along with a plethora of varying cultures such as Celtic, Greek, and Roman Gods and Goddesses who individually rule over different dominions—each have different-colored skin and speak varying languages of the world. Along with the differing dominions of faith, each religion houses "their" God in a church, a temple, or a hall of congregation to worship that which is "unreachable" from self alone.

Predominantly, religion has mankind congregating in its own divergent parishes and empires built of mortar and stone, with churches that are largely tied into a qualifying monetary system.

The more offerings and donations made, the more accolades are given to those who give, with closer admittance to the access to the higher echelons of religious order.

The miracle of life and creation, of which many refer to its maker by the many names of God, has created the most beautiful house of prayer for humankind, with an altar at every footstep along the way. We can walk in reverence with the ground under our feet, look up to the expanse of the sky, be shaded under a tree, wash our worries in the rivers, lakes and oceans. We can listen to the sermons of the natural world. Isn't the place of our God-given abode in a natural world enough? Perhaps because the natural world is equally free for all, it is held in less regard and value by such hierological orders?

Religion limits the infinite and boundless energy of our Creator into separate houses, each with distinct dominions, and adorned with icons and idols that "represent" the All That Is. In the common sense of ultimate truth, these icons are, in fact, false idols (something deemed illegitimate), that are man-made ornaments to fashionably decorate the "house of God." How could a building filled with religious effigies represent the Absolute or possibly override the importance of our Creator's making?

Clergymen and priests have wedged themselves between our solemn and sovereign rights to connect with the supreme Godhead within ourselves at any time and any place. This "holds" the intimate connection with God behind the closed doors of our minds and hearts and vacant from the holy house within each and every one of us. One illustration of this is that a newborn is deemed sanctified and absolved from sin only once it is baptized and only then. It is the newborn that baptizes us with its innate innocence, free from the stigma of guilt and wrongfulness. Its purity and divinity bless us with love that comes directly from the Source of Love itself. Direct union and communion with the Divine are disavowed unless bridged by the clergymen of a religious order.

This seed of separation and segregation is inculcated from the seed of its inception of "Original Sin" in the Garden of Eden. We were taught that men and women will not see eye to eye and that women are the weaker gender that succumb to their own whims. That if you exercise your own choice, you are not worthy of living in the Garden of Life, and have to obey the rules or you WILL be ostracized, penalized, and suffer the penalty of banishment from the Divine. That it is the woman's fault that man has to toil in the fields with sweat on his brow because it was Eve that ate the forbidden fruit. In the eyes of the early Christian religion, it was Eve's fault that we are in the state we are in today and that the connection to a beautiful life of abundance is lost. Didn't Adam eat the apple too?

We see the separation and segregation that religion lends itself to in fighting wars in the name of religion, along with the sexual covertness and lawlessness that take place behind the cloistered walls that deem to separate man from God.

Even though religion has constructed walls of separation and segregation in serving the greater congregation of humankind, it can serve as a source of comfort and guidance to the populace, providing a basis for moral beliefs and behaviors. It can also support a sense of community and connection to tradition. It should not, however, indoctrinate and segregate people from their original birthright to feel, think, and stand in their own stream of consciousness and connection to the Divine.

With spirituality on the other hand, while it may portray its own varying levels of colors and textures, it encompasses and embraces all legions of faith and practices, no matter what creed or culture, under one roof of sky, soul, and universe. Spirituality of secular faith belongs not to one single dominion alone but honors all faiths—Buddhism, Islam, Judaism, Native American, Hindu, Celtic, and then some— and at its cornerstone are the practices centered within the embodiment of love, unity, and peace. Phonetically speaking, the word "spiritual" then becomes "Spirit You All." In that it embraces the spirit of The ALL in our practice; that we are not separate from the spiritual realms of love, unity, and peace that reside in the temple within...for the body is one of the purest expressions of God there is.

The pathway of spirituality rests in prayer and meditation, yoga, walking, and contemplating the entirety of the universe in the natural world of life itself. Whether it is under a roof, on the ground, in nature, or in the simple act of eating and bathing, it is already rooted within your natural birthright. To connect to the Divine, to God, to the Mother, to the Father, the Maker-Creator or the Universe, all are sacred elements in the grand wheel of life.

The prayer that flows from your heart is in each footstep within the living mandala of life. The trees that connect with each other through their roots, the standing stones, the elements of the Earth that work in perfect unison for all of life, the animals, the humans, the angels, and the like, are all sacred. Each are the direct living expressions of God in the Garden of Eden.

The spirit of the stones in the hills of New Mexico knew that we are all connected in the congregation of all of life when they informed me in one of my rock retrievals I undertook:

> *"A bit like you humans. Even though you have individual heads, your own arms and legs, YOU ARE TRAVELING UNDER ONE HUMAN SKIN!"*

They, along with all of Mother Nature, offer us the sermons of truth and wisdom, speaking to us in the sacred knowledge of the Divine, of the Universe, Creator Mother-Father God. This sacred language shows and teaches us that everything has its divine purpose and that not one thing is more valid and divine than the other. Not one faith is more valid or divine than each other. Each living thing weaves its threads into the greater tapestry with God in the center and heart of every living atom. Herein lies spirituality.

In proportion to the broader scale of beliefs, religion, we could say, "is the one inch" of which spirituality is the "whole nine yards." Religion exemplifies the separate puzzle pieces and spirituality reveals the entire puzzle in one unified field.

Spirituality connects us to a state of being that is more concerned with the human spirit and soul. It connects us more deeply with our individual practice and belief within the naturalness of the environment and of self within.

There are many roads that can lead us to the top of the mountain. We each have the choice as to which path we take. Ultimately, it is the intent and purity of heart from which we choose that can make the difference.

ACTIVATION

Where does the altar of God reside within your own being? Do you see God/Creator outside of yourself, above in the heavens? Or in the trees, in the flowers, in a smile, or in a newborn's eye? Do you speak or make prayers to something outside of yourself, or do you feel the power of prayer within as already God-given?

Contemplate these questions to recognize what feels "right" for you within your own heart and soul.

The Way of the Phoenix

Many of us know of the Phoenix, not just as the city of Arizona, U.S.A., or as the name of a sports team, but also in the recesses of history as a mythological creature/bird. It is regarded as a bird of legend of immense power, alchemy, immortality, renewal and resurrection. It is a fabled, legendary being that rises to the occasion, and flies higher still, until it combusts in its own flames, crashes to the ground, dies and is reborn anew from its own ashes.

This legendary creature demonstrates the power to surge to the ultimate heights and also plummet to the rock-bottom low. The phoenix exemplifies the principle of alchemy: an ancient chemical and transmutational process of changing base metals, such as lead, into noble metals such as gold.

Or, on a more spiritual, philosophical level, this powerful mythical bird transforms from one base level of existence—of destruction and demise—to higher planes of existence—such as elation and exaltation. It symbolizes the alchemical transfiguration process of giving rise to life after death and personifies immortality with the life-death-life cycle, where the end is only the beginning.

The proverb, "To rise like a phoenix from the ashes," means to emerge from adversity or a catastrophe much stronger, smarter and more powerful, with a renewed sense of unleashed power. Just like the phoenix bird that cycles from one death-defying state to another of renewed life, we can also adopt its magical capacity to harness our power, resurrect beyond our limitations and challenging circumstances, and rise into a new life-affirmed state.

We can let go of the old to make way for the new; we can release old habits, harmful thoughts, limiting beliefs and former patterns that no longer serve us for our highest good. Like the phoenix, we can burn these away by expressing and releasing our anger, rage, exasperations and frustrations of negative cycles that need to be uplifted from our downfalls. We can utilize the intensity of our emotions that can otherwise consume us, by burning them away into a pile of ashes that gives rise to the new embers of creation.

How do we do this effectively without hurting ourselves or others?

We can channel this raw, fiery energy in a respectful, effective and appropriate way by dancing it out, running it out, boxing, kickboxing, skipping, breathwork, chopping wood, or using the energy creatively or constructively in building something like a house. There are even places you can go called "rage rooms" where you can "thrash it out" and let go of your pent-up emotions by smashing plates, crockery and glassware! The expression of this kind of unleashed energy needs to match the power of the emotion you are feeling. In other words, it won't work so well to circumvent your anger, passion, or fiery energy within by smiling it away, affirming it away, or by spiritually bypassing it. Yes, we can elevate our emotions to a higher spiritual level by embracing them without judgment and with pure awareness. However, most of us are not yet fully adept at doing so and will need the physical release in order to move the energy to a higher plane. Either way, we need to accept these feelings and honor them by giving them a voice, by expressing them in a safe container and in a conscious, healing manner.

Many of the Light Workers who came into this incarnation to bring light into the darkness, to bring consciousness into unconsciousness, to bring love into realms of fear did not have the space in their childhood to feel safe to express anger or to exercise their boundaries and say NO!

Fortunately, the "terrible twos" granted release for many through their tantrums as they gathered up all their pent-up frustrations, tensed up and held their breath to then let it all out in one long scream.

Others like myself were not allowed to express such fiery emotions. It's not what a good girl would do. It is very important that we release what does not serve us in order to rise out of the darkness into light, out of unconsciousness into conscious awareness and from fear into love, which is our spiritual plight.

By expressing and releasing intense emotions such as fear, lack, insecurity, jealousy, or even extreme sensations that come with abounding joy and elation, we can discharge the energy that was otherwise trapped in the body. Thus, it creates and allows a new surge of energy that we can then utilize and channel into a new project, a new direction, and a new and fresh outlook that creates a higher state of life. This unleashed energy gives fuel for our flight out of the darkened cinder state to higher ground, just like the phoenix demonstrates.

How can we rise out of our own ashes?

If you have crashed and burned, allow yourself to feel the death of the old along with the surrender of "letting it all go." It is important to honor the passage of death in the form of sadness, momentary defeat, or of hopelessness. However, we don't stay there, indulge our ego and identify with the misery that can keep us in the ashes longer than we need.

The ashes are the remains and cremains of our old ways, of toxic emotional waste, of that which no longer serves our growth. By giving them credence and freeing up the energy in your mind and body, this waste matter gets converted into the very fertilizer and fuel that gives us the energy of propulsion to surge out of our demise and forge into the emergence of the new.

We must embrace that we are ourselves first—creatures of the Earth—and must embrace and release our base, primal emotions such as anger, insecurity and competition in order to evolve into the higher realms of being. This allows the kundalini—the Life Force Energy—that has been kept in the basement of our being to rise up and out of our lower base chakras where our fears, insecurities and animal emotions are often hidden, denied and repressed. By expressing them appropriately, we release the energy into the higher chakras, where it can be repurposed for new ways of thinking and seeing more clearly into the higher state of our human evolution.

The phoenix, a fabled bird, remains to this day alive in our heart and mind. It is a great teacher, reminding us of the eternal cycle of release and renewal, of life eternal, of the cycle of death and rebirth within the Self.

ACTIVATION

How do you bypass your base feelings?

How does this inhibit or prevent new outcomes in your life?

In which ways can you express these pent-up feelings to let your inner creature/bird raise to new heights?

Passion Prayers of Manifestation

As children, we knew how to dream. We could spend countless hours looking up to the sky and daydreaming of one day becoming a movie star, an astronaut, a doctor, or a teacher.

The imagination ran wild, untethered from any form of inhibition or limitation. Whatever it was that we dreamed of, we saw it, we felt it, we were *in* it. We *were* it.

The body itself is like a child. Innocently, and without judgment, it takes the instructions of thought and starts to put it into action. So, whatever we think in that moment, we begin to *become* in that moment.

Very often in my healing practice, I use a process of which I ask my client to think of a negative experience, whether it was recent or in the distant past. After only thirty seconds, I ask them what they felt in their body.

They normally begin by saying they felt an overall sense of contraction and tension, their breathing held in or shortened, their heart closing in or feeling heavy, and their energy plummeting downward.

In the next moment, when I ask them to focus on a positive thought or experience, the complete opposite is felt. The chest and breathing open, there is a sense of lightness in the heart, and an overall calmness spreads throughout the entire body.

Our body responds to every single thought via our highly attuned nervous system. In other words, we feel our thoughts.

We have all experienced a sleeping dream at one time or another, where we are fully immersed in the dream as if we are there and feeling the living sensations of it. When we wake up, we feel as if we lived it in real life. We may still be reeling from the sensations and blush when we bump into the person we may have experienced an intimate moment with in the dream. Our mind does not distinguish reality from illusion. The dream then becomes a part of our living body experience.

The energy of the Universe, like our mind/body complex, is also a conscious field that is alive and awake. It responds to us in every moment, weaving our thought forms into the fabric of living existence. Being made of the same energy, we are integrated into the mind of the Universe so that when we think a thought, it responds like our nervous system and complies without judgment to generate our thoughts into matter.

Understanding this, we can start to flesh out our dreams and aspirations to bring more substance to them with the cooperation and co-creation of the Universe. We can dream like we did as children—with full mind/thought, full body/feeling with eagerness and spiritedness—with passion as the driving force, the e-motion (energy in motion) to drive the intention into creation. Passion is the fuel that propels our dreams into the realm of possibility. It brings belief and faith into the forefront of vision and follows through all the way down into the embodiment, into the concretization of a dream made manifest.

It is not enough to just *think* of something flippantly and expect it to materialize. Nor is it enough that we just keep on asking for the same thing over and over again. Our prayers and dreams need to be founded and grounded in our bodies. As we anchor our prayers in the material plane, so they shall be returned to us in the physical. They won't be left groundless, suspended like pies in the sky.

The trouble is, we have such scattered brains that we are in constant flux with what we desire, and the universal field has to chase our thoughts around. More often than not, our dreams don't get realized because they could not take root in the field of possibility.

Remember that it is the *passion* felt in the body, in conjunction with the thought and felt as though it is already done, which supplies the fuel that rocket-ships the dream and pierces the veils of illusion and creation.

I experienced a miraculous event that gave me solid confirmation of this knowing:

I was walking the land and caught my thoughts slowly plunging into a familiar furrow of doubt and uncertainty. I had not felt this for a long while, but here it was rearing its head again. The feeling of heaviness grew, along with the sense of lack and dullness. But instead of letting it take me all the way down into the trench of scarcity and inadequacy, I caught the pathway my ego had often taken before and saw the pothole I need not fall into.

I stopped in my tracks, which put a full stop to my thinking process. My mind became clear and ready for something new. With my feet planted strongly and firmly on the ground, I said, "Hey, wait a minute! I am amazing. Look what I have accomplished in my life. I am a wonderful person. I am honest, hard-working, funny, intelligent, and wise." I raised my arms up into the clear blue sky like a tree with my roots anchored to Mother Earth, and with fierce intention I summoned up the truth of my totality. Passion was full speed ahead with all the might I could muster, ready to tear through the universal fabric, to be heard once and for all.

"Why is it that I attract money and abundance easily and effortlessly? How is it that money flows so easily to me while doing the things I love best?" I felt this prayer in the asking as if I already had it and became it and saw the money flowing toward me. I was smiling with a sense of content, fulfillment, and glee. I knew that if I asked the universe a question, it must reply with an answer. But I never in a million years expected my answer to be returned so soon.

Five minutes later, as I walked off the trail and onto a footpath around a clubhouse, I saw a white envelope faced

*down on the ground. I picked it up and what was in the
envelope? It was money! Not just a few bills, but a full envelope
filled with eight 100-dollar bills. I was astounded!*

"It couldn't work that fast, could it?" Oh yes, it can!

*It was clear validation from the Universe that the Law of
Attraction can work swiftly when you add the essential
components of passion with seeing, feeling, and believing to the
equation. I did hand it in to the police station, but made sure
that I let Spirit know in gratitude that I received the affirmation
of abundance first. It was retrieved by the owner, who gave
me a lovely reward of 100 dollars and made me a beautiful
shaman's talking stick that I continue to use with the blessing
of the universe in my healing sessions.*

As we were growing up, we were taught to pray to God for something
that we would wish to come true. Our asking and pleading were
sent outwardly from us to a higher force. As we continued to direct
our energy outwardly, it kept us in the loop of "wanting mode" and
"not having" mode. No matter how hard we wished for it, "it" often
remained suspended somewhere in space, out of our range.

When we add passion and vision to our prayer by not only seeing it but *feeling* it as if it is already present within us, we are em-
bodying our prayer. Our mind believes it has happened, our body
responds in gratitude and appreciation, and the Universe complies
to bring it into the physical. This is a simple Law of the Universe
that is applicable to our living reality.

It may not happen instantaneously for you like it did with me on
the land. You may need to imagine (image-in) your vision with more
consistency for it to open to the field of your dreams. You may need
to add even more passion—more wood on the fire—to intensify the
burning desire to create and to keep your dream-prayer fully alive
and lit.

Creation and manifestation cannot just be a trick of the mind or
a mere mental exercise. It is not as easy as sitting back and letting it
happen. It takes divine intention that necessitates passion as the fuel

which drives the energy toward the manifestation of our dreams and prayers.

It is no wonder why we have been steered away from passion and desire, as they are usually deemed as "non-spiritual" and less virtuous aspects of ourselves, lest we become self-satisfying heathens. The higher dimension of passion as a generative force in the living field of creation is as spiritual as it gets.

ACTIVATION

What is it that you wish to bring home to yourself? Sit quietly and allow yourself to dream your vision.

SEE it like a preview of a movie. See the colors, the shapes.

SMELL the aromas.

TASTE the experience.

FEEL the sensations and immerse yourself in this vision as if it is already done and you are *living* the dream.

Now add the burning desire of PASSION to the mix. Breathe it all the way into your heart and embrace it with glee. Give thanks for it already being created in this moment.

The joy of your body and the universe applaud you in the power of dreaming your dream awake.

WISDOM

Finally, the Wisdom section invites us to bridge the gamut of Earth and Spirit so that we may ground the mind into our bodies and into our heart-knowing. This invites us to embody the teachings, stay in our center lane and return to our alignment with our greater sense of self. In effect, to become an Antenna of Spirit.

Presence as the
Art of Being

• Whatever life presents to you has come about for a higher reason and purpose. Life is not challenging you. Instead, it brings forth the perfect scenario and outcome to reflect and mirror your energy and what you are streaming forth into the Universe in each moment.

Whether the glass is half full or half empty is contingent on the observer. When we deem a situation as hurtful or discouraging, leaving us feeling betrayed, ashamed, guilty, alone, unworthy or afraid, we combat the situation by blaming "the other" to disqualify these feelings. When we blame and shame the other, we are not taking responsibility for our feelings—for what we create and put out there in our lives. This perpetuates a never-ending loop of further pushing our power away from ourselves, leaving us feeling even more helpless and shaming ourselves.

We do have the ability to respond in a new way that can bring us to higher ground. Rather than discrediting ourselves and thrusting our feelings back into recession, we are invited to reclaim our power and light by breathing into the heavy feelings of shame and guilt as a call to action. This lessens the burden and lightens the load to free the body and mind from the grip of trauma.

Give yourself the opportunity to let go by taking a full inhale into these dense feelings, followed by a big exhale to release them from your body. Your feelings are like little children who want and need your attention. The more you ignore them, the more they will tug at you until you take notice. All they really want is to be listened to, acknowledged and accepted. By breathing into and taking responsibility for your feelings without the shame and blame, the wounded child within is not sent further into the darkness where it is unheard, alone and separate, but acknowledged and embraced and brought forth into the light of your loving awareness.

If you breathe into your feelings—whether they are of pain or pleasure, of shame or innocence—into the parts of you that you judge as well as the parts of you that you celebrate, and just feel it in presence without judgment, you are living life to the fullest!

Let us take a look at what happens when we hold our breath in the contraction of fear and fright:

Let's say you are driving along the road and an animal runs out in front of your car unexpectedly. What is the first thing that happens? You might say that you put on the brakes. But the very first thing that happens is that you inhale a sharp short gasp, tense up and contract your muscles. Then the brakes are slammed, simultaneously holding in the trauma and fright within the held breath.

Thereafter, what would we need to do to let go of the fright from our bodies? We would need to take a very conscious outward breath—an *exhale*—to let go of the fright and panic from the body. Then we could take a few more conscious breaths straight after to clear the fright out so that it doesn't get pushed down into the deeper strata of the body.

The Body acts as a repository; a storehouse that records memories of past experiences in the muscles. This is called *muscle memory*. This is how the physique of the body can be misshaped and distorted by the contraction of musculature over the years, and also how our facial lines can reveal the longstanding emotions held in the muscles of the face.

Let us not burden the body or mind with past hurts and experiences, but rather breathe into the feelings and then release them from your body with an exhale. We take our first inhale at birth and our last exhale at death, which illustrates that we inhale to feel life and we exhale to let it all go.

When we stop breathing, we ultimately die. When we breathe more, we essentially feel more alive.

How can we deal with buried pain?

This was astounding to me to understand this Body Wisdom. I have come to the conclusion that there is only one way to move through pain, whether it be physical or emotional, and that is to *feel it*! Pain needs to be felt without judging or resisting it, and to be fully accepted as part of the transfiguration process of healing. In order to be forged into our true might, we are challenged to walk through the alchemical fires to transmute density into light.

I came across this realization during one unforgettable night in the Yucatán, Mexico. My right-side wisdom tooth had become inflamed over the course of several weeks and it was time for an extraction. I had put off the idea of going to a dentist until I returned to the United States. But the pain had exacerbated, and it was 3:00 in the morning, while the whole town was asleep.

With no one to reach out to, no cell phone with me, and not knowing the language proficiently enough to speak to hotel management, I felt alone, as if I was the only one alive in the world in the dead of night. The tooth pain was screeching, piercing my brain; it took me over. I did not take painkillers as my path as a naturopathic doctor knew that my body was doing the right thing and that instead of suppressing what my body was expressing, I was to stay present with it. I always trust in my body; it never lies and does not ever lead me astray. *Let me be present with the pain,* I thought. I knew that feelings are like small children pulling on my apron strings, that there is something they need that I am not paying attention to. I had, for a long time, resisted most of my feelings in my life and had learned that if I listen intently, they would have messages for me I need to heed.

Staggering with pain like a drunkard to the rooftop of the hotel where the full moon shone so brightly, blaring at me, everything seemed exaggerated. I closed my eyes and focused on my paining tooth. I sat to listen to what it was saying to me about the wisdom I had gleaned over the years and not to impact the wisdom by suppressing it but rather share it with the world.

I traveled into the core of the pain, spiraling inward to the epicenter, and right there in the center point—the bull's eye—I found something very interesting! I reached the eye of the storm, where it was calm. There was no pain, no resistance, but right there at the center rested pure *sensation*. Sensation, without labeling or judging it as pain or pleasure, as something wrong or right, did not permit it to become an emotion but was left untouched as pure sensation.

Pure Life Force coursed through me like a freight train. There was nowhere to cling to, nowhere to add on to, nowhere to turn, nothing but feeling the abounding energy running through my body. Going back to the very epicenter of the pain led me back to a sensation of the origin place of primeval energy.

I had traveled back through the wormhole of living presence, where there is no past to hold on to or future to step into...only pure presence! I had arrived at the pre-sense that reaches the body in living awareness without resistance and without judgment. Perhaps this is where Christ had come to on the crucifix? In forging forgiveness at the mercy of pain, he transcended pain and traveled into the pre-sense of the Divine.

We need not resist pain nor pleasure. Instead, we could take a deeper dive into the interiors of our Body Wisdom to listen and learn from it. We can take the opportunity to lift our trials and tribulations to the next level of initiation, to raise the cross toward exaltation, beyond pain or pleasure, beyond this or that.

When we feel the pure sensation as it is, we free it back into existence.

ACTIVATION

Try this approach the next time you experience the discomfort of pain, whether it be emotional or physical. Rather than trying to work out what is wrong, take a deep breath into the sensation and allow it to be just as it is without trying to dismiss or negate it. Listen to and tune into what the body is asking of you, like you would a child tugging at you for attention. Continue to inhale deeply and let go on each exhale as you hone into the epicenter to see if you can relax into the pure energy of the sensation where presence resides.

Our Diamond Self

Like diamonds, our being reflects and refracts the pure light that lies deep within its subterranean levels. They remind us to rise up out of these depths and reveal the twinkle of our soul's light that every one of us holds. As multidimensional beings comprised of light-filled particles, the color of our expressions is reflected from each of the manifold facets of Self.

Natural diamonds require specific conditions of 90–125 miles below the Earth's mantle—where the temperatures are at least 2,000 degrees—with carbon, water, and maximal pressure needed to form them. It takes billions of years for carbon, the foundation of all life in the world around us, to crystallize in the form of a diamond. They are then delivered to Earth's surface during deep-source volcanic eruptions, which carry the diamonds rapidly to the surface.

Born from the dark bowels of the earth, diamonds show us that from the deepest depth of our being—and under the intensity and pressures we undergo—we, too, can raise our brilliance to the surface in the full spectrum of light.

Derived from the Greek words "Adamas," meaning "unbreakable and/or invincible," and "Diaphanous," meaning "transparent"—diamonds, from their hardness and deep-rooted strength, can cut through concrete, stone, steel, and other metals. Their strength, along with their sharp edges, demonstrates how we can also call on our inner durability and fortitude to cut through the falsity with our clarity. We can carve through illusions to enter into the light of truth, into the transparency of any given situation.

In this time of our evolution, we are asked to condense our purpose of being, to not waste our time in idleness, but to cut to the chase, and to "see into" the transparency of truth that can radiate the light of our brilliance into the dark recesses of history.

It is no wonder why these precious stones have been regarded over centuries as gems that bear longevity and dependability, which are given as a betrothal proclamation for the longstanding promise of love and hope for a brighter future.

Their blinding beauty and illustrious brilliance catch the eye with prismatic light that casts all colors of the rainbow from every multifaceted angle. Each window reveals the inner mansions of clarity, strength, and precision.

We have been led to believe that we are composed of separate parts of ourselves, each pushing and fighting to shine more brightly than the other. We have forgotten that we are a whole diamond that shines at every angle and at every turn. Each facet of ourselves faces its own way and yet is connected to the entirety of self.

We must appreciate the precious gem we each are and behold ourselves as a natural wonder of the world. We must not feign our intrinsic value, for our eminence lies deep within. It is time to turn our inner eye into our light-filled consciousness, toward our Diamond Self.

There you are.

ACTIVATION

In a quiet moment of introspection, see yourself as a sparkling, prismatic diamond. See it encompassing and extending around your entire body. Bring into your awareness the multitude of aspects of yourself—all the virtues, your strengths, your courage, your tenacity and brilliance.

Call on the sun to shine upon you as you turn the diamond slowly. See and feel each side revealing and radiating its pure light in full admiration. Are there any facets still hidden in the dark? If so, turn your inner diamond to let the light shine upon it and within it.

All aspects of you get to shine once they are seen and appreciated.

Focus Your Attention
and Hone In

My first introduction to "the power of focusing my attention" was in a pottery class at Moorabbin Technical College in Melbourne, Australia. Mrs. White was my instructor, and she was teaching us how to throw clay on a wheel to make our first clay pot. This was going to be a new experience for me, and I was eager to learn.

First up, we were instructed to knead the ball of clay to get all the air bubbles out and to combine the minerals in the clay evenly and smoothly. I knew how to knead dough for making bread, and this was exactly the same, so I was off to a good start. I was feeling confident, bordering on the side of cocky, as I threw the clay on the steel revolving wheel with full force to make it stick.

This is going to be easy! I thought. The dank smell of wet earth and the sound of the revolving wheels filled the pottery room. The boys were chuckling at the girls as we were seriously focused on our mission.

It was only a few moments after I wrapped my hands around the clay before it haphazardly escaped my hands, flung off the wheel with a diagonal thrust, and clung itself to the wall. I laughed raucously as I had never seen such a thing.

I confidently prized the lump of clay off the wall and started the procedure again. I figured it would take more concentration the second time around. But that didn't help; the clay had its way with me once more as it flew off the wheel and plastered itself onto the wall again.

I laughed loudly and heartily in amazement that I, who was so confident, couldn't achieve what seemed like a simple act. I again prized the clay off the wall, this time feeling a little undermined that it may have a mind of its own and that it may be more powerful than mine.

I took a deep breath and threw what now felt like something that may just be unmanageable on the rotating wheel one more time with all my might of attention so that it would not escape the confines of my hands. Mrs. White came and stood behind me, placed her hands over mine for guidance, and whispered, "You need to *focus your attention*. Draw your elbows into your body and let the power from within extend from your belly and out through your arms."

I did exactly what she instructed. I focused my attention on the smoothened clay as it whirled between my hands and held my elbows into my torso so that my arms and hands extended from a sturdy and stable place. From there I let the energy stream up from my belly. Instantaneously, the clay rose up between my hands from a lump on the wheel and like magic, it grew into a perfectly even, tall, uniform column. Then, as I placed my thumb in the center, it opened into a vase...*my* vase!

That's when it happened! As the clay was rising upward, growing taller from the base, something also arose within me. Was it my confidence? My capability? From struggle to ease, from failure to success, from a lump of clay into an earthen pot, I became energized and enlivened, my spine snapped into straightness, and my sight sharpened. Could it have been my Life Force? Was it the awakening of my kundalini energy that lay dormant at the base of the spine that had risen out of its slumber? This natural Life Force Energy that derived from a deeper place of origin wanted to flow up and out, to be released into creation.

This experience was a true initiation into my spiritual life, introducing to me the power of our own internal energy that wants to manifest into being. Just like the lump of clay, I rose out of my body into something more, something higher!

I had a realization that we are more than the physical. We are made of Spirit, of Life Force Energy that desires to experience itself in the physical.

I was given a new directive to live my life: *to focus my attention and hone in*. Do not give up on the first round, the second or the third; something or someone will come to your aid and show you how to do it.

I learned to slow down, focus and hone in, lest things run amok!

In sharpening your mind of awareness to bring forth your manifestation, *focusing your attention* is necessary. In order to harness your willpower and exercise the muscle of diligence and tenacity, you must stick with it; pull it up from the ground of your being and out into the world. You will see and know there is something deeper in you that can arise with this willful force that is there to help you along the way.

ACTIVATION

Is there a desire within you that wants to arise out of dormancy? Is there a part of you that wants to find more of your confidence, your willpower, more love of self, or something you are creating?

Focus your attention and hone into that urge. Call upon your Life Force Energy to accompany it, to give it the fuel it needs to rise and ascend into its greater expression of itself.

The Arrow of Intention

We pull back on our arrow with a tight grip and hold it back when we live life in contraction or fear. In fearfulness, we restrain our arrow from being released from our grasp much longer than needed. It is from this place of trepidation that when flung loose, our arrow of intention propels with an equal and opposite direction and with force, straight into the epicenter, into the bullseye of fear itself.

It is important to realize that our thoughts work much the same way. They are themselves like arrows that are flung from our minds and projected out into the space before us, into the field of consciousness. As the Universe responds by manifesting thought/energy into action/matter, it is important to focus our thoughts with resolute intention and aim them toward where we do want them to go rather than where we don't want them to go.

We need not withdraw our energy from situations and others through fear, but learn how to use our bows and arrows wisely and effectively and from a place of calm confidence. It takes diligence, along with a stance of commitment, to stand steady on the ground of possibility and belief. To pull your arrow firmly back into your bow from this unwavering stance allows you to aim more carefully and consciously toward your target goal or intention.

While the tip of each arrow must be aimed with the correct intention and focus to reach its intended target, the tail of each arrow has feathers that help it to fly. Our prayers, thoughts and intentions are carried along with the feathers to forge their way through time and space into its manifested outcome.

The arrow of consciousness is not something to be trigger-happy with, but asks us to become masters of conscious archery and to pull in our arrow of thought/energy first, with a sense of self-command, before releasing it to the Universe to be made manifest. Let's not forget that the more we pull our arrow back, the more momentum it has to reach its target, lest our arrow drops short of the distance and misses the mark.

Are you directing your energy and staying the course?

If for example, you are wishing to attract a loving and committed relationship, it is required that you harness your energy and pull it back a little so you don't leak your energy this way and that—so that you are not jumping into a half-hearted relationship with this person or the next. It is important to give yourself patience and time so that when you let your arrow go, it arrives at its destination point with your prayer of love and clear vision. Otherwise, you may end up in a field of strewn arrows on the ground before you—arrows that did not make their marks, leaving you with disappointment and a sense of disillusionment with your efforts.

Or perhaps your aim is to diligently save your money for a nest egg or to build or buy a home. It is required of you to focus your energy and thoughts toward this goal. Pulling back from spending your money unwisely on large, unnecessary purchases can diminish your energy and time, leaving you with limited funds to bank on what you truly wish for.

So instead of expending your energy on the things you don't need or want, become in charge of your energy, so you can direct your arrows of intention into what you are truly holding out for.

ACTIVATION

Take a few moments to see and feel what it is that you truly wish to focus your energy and intentions toward. If you have some arrows strewn on the ground before you, pick them up and put them back in your harness.

Visualize yourself standing grounded with a firm stance and with your arrow of intention pulled back into you. Feel the focus of your intentional energy and gather your might and hold your arrow strong with calm confidence and you will know when is the right time to let your arrow release toward its mark.

Dialing the Right Number

We need to dial the right number to reach the person we are wishing to speak with. We cannot tap a random number on our phones and expect to reach the person we are calling. The same applies to connecting to radio and television stations we are interested in listening to or watching. There is a specific bandwidth we need to reach in order to tune into the channel we desire.

Each of us has a specific frequency that needs to be tapped into if we are to truly connect with one another. If someone is hypersensitive, we need to attune to that sensitivity to reach that person's level of receivership. If they are quiet and demure, then we may need to turn our volume down a little to match their level of comfort. We also know this as "matching their energy" or "striking a rapport." Others may call it "harmonizing" with each other. In the end, it is about creating a safe container from which more trust can build, where the energy between you can find a place of comfort and connection. As we are each unique with our own individual personalities, there is a broad range of channels from which we can tap into.

Within ourselves too, we need to focus in and fine-tune our thoughts to that which we desire to bring forth in our lives. If we wish to attract Love in our lives, then it stands to reason that we set our inner dials to the awareness, and emotional energy and vibration of Love. Attuning to the frequency, and harmonizing and matching the energy of Love, allows us to become a transmission of Love, thereby having it reflected back to us as part of the universal Law of Attraction.

Most of us fear Love, however. Our undermining shadow tells us that we are unlovable and not good enough to have it in our lives. It also tells us that we need to overcompensate for the lack we feel by broadcasting our best image of ourselves to the outside world, thus shielding the vulnerability needed to open our heart to this vibration. Our excessive and unbridled thoughts create static noise, blotting out the reception, making it more challenging to hone in and focus with clarity on the station we wish to tune into.

We have become very accustomed to this static activity of the mind as normalcy and have forgotten that underneath the chatter and noise is clarity, peace, and quiet. Our dials are way off—and it is up to each and every one of us to set them straight and fine-tune our awareness through the continuous practice of quietude and centeredness. This helps us dial into the inner station of peace and calm to feel the love within.

As we hone into the quieter and more peaceful channels, we can harmonize with the transmission they offer, which can entrain us to a higher frequency. This attunement sets the dial in the right direction, allowing us to feel the love or whatever it is your heart desires, which sets the motion of attracting "the likeness and reflection of your desire" right back to you.

ACTIVATION

Watch your mind with the passing thoughts like the static you hear searching for a clear station on a radio. Listen for the silent and clear points along the way. Hone in on these quieter points to attune to the peace and calm, so you can visualize and feel more clearly what you truly wish to attract and manifest in your life.

Chasing the
Dragon's Tail

If your mind is vacillating, your thoughts thrashing about, perhaps you are chasing the dragon's tail! No sooner do we find ourselves in a tailspin, as we grapple to grab the tail and hang on for dear life, when it flips to the other side with a thud! We hang on even tighter until we are thrust to the other side, back and forth.

When we chase our circumstances from one idea to the next, from one situation to the next, from one person to the next, in order to tame and control the outcomes in our lives, we are undoubtedly chasing the dragon's tail! "If only I can be stronger and not react; if I could just take a bold stand and confront the situation head-on; if I would dress more attractively, get a stylish haircut, be more open and vulnerable, not express my feelings as much, give more of myself, become more mysterious, or work a little harder in order to achieve what I want in my life..." We have been programmed to think that we can do more, achieve more, strive more or go the extra mile to create the outcomes we desire.

We are seduced by form with the propensity to change the scene, demand behavioral changes of others, relocate to another country, or replace people in our lives to bring about the results we desire.

We are human beings, not human doings. We have been caught in the net of neo-slavery, with the belief that the more we do, the more we achieve and the more we spend the more we are fulfilled. It is true that our society is run on this basis. We get paid for putting in more hours, we get accoladed for the financial abundance we've gained, but at the end of the day, it is how you are left feeling that matters. After all the darn hard work you have put into your career, your family, your relationship, your looks, your home, your security—at the end of the day, at the end of your life, how do you feel? Are you feeling fulfilled? Are you feeling loved? Are you in full knowing of who you truly are?

At the end of it all, it is not about how much you have achieved, but who you have become in the process. In the deeper-down place of your being, are you free of lurking fears and is the dragon still menacing you?

When we blame others, or the places we live in, or assign our power over to governments and authorities, we are powerless to change. We are flipped and lashed around on the dragon's tail in the process, making it even more unclear as to how we could possibly master the situation at hand and make true headway.

Let go of the tail. Stand back for a minute and take a good look at how you may have lost your balance, your right seeing, your true vision. Everything you see is a result of your thoughts. Rightful seeing does not happen from trying to control and tranquilize the dragon, but rather to see and witness what you deem and think about yourself and about your life.

Your thoughts create your feelings that are then harbored within your body. Watching, witnessing, feeling and accepting what we have created in our lives is how to tame your inner dragon. The True Self is tugging at you for attention to correct your stance and balance. Our tendency is to run from our inner feelings, as we just don't want to feel pain and discomfort; we've had enough of it in our lives! The feelings we judge as hurtful and negative get pushed down into the caverns of our minds and deeper into our bodies as we endeavor to mitigate them under the guise of having to get the job done. This leaves us no time to stop and keep the pace on the treadmill.

Our feelings can tell us a lot about what we say and have repeatedly told ourselves over the years. Emotions such as excitement, sadness, happiness, joy, rejection, loneliness, and curiosity are the expressions of an energy we have harnessed in our lives. Our thoughts produce a set of chemicals that are expressed and released within the body, with each changing thought. Our thoughts generate beliefs that we then act upon and come to believe are true, that this is how it works. It is solely up to us to manage, feel them and let them go as they arise if we are to feel the free flow of unhindered Life Force throughout our bodies.

A powerful teacher of mine in Australia by the name of David Ward once taught me that "feelings are sensations, and emotions are feelings with a judgment attached to them." He also said that "the only cause of physical pain is the resistance to feeling" and "the only cause of emotional pain is judgment." In its pure sense, sensations are how the body processes the chemistry and energy running through it. Hot-heated, intense, contractive, faster and shorter breaths are sensations that more likely reflect anger and frustration, and open, cool, expanded sensations more likely reflect peace and calm.

The body never lies about such things, it is a reliable source to check in about how you are thinking, believing, and managing your energy. It is important to stop, even if for a moment, to give credence to your feelings, to observe them, feel and accept them as they are, and embrace them without judgment. As long as we can accept the feelings and emotions that we ourselves have cultivated, we have the power to change them.

After all, feelings are parts of the self that are calling for attention to be invited into the fold, into the arms of your loving self. Behind these feelings is the quiet space of your own inner spirit that has solutions and wisdom that can help you along your way. It is therefore imperative that we give ourselves time for meditation and contemplation to reset our chemistry, rebalance our energy, and return to innocence in body, mind and spirit. Life has a great way of getting you to feel what you have been denying, so it's best to tune into your feeling-body and keep it flowing; to learn to walk in harmony or in step with our greater self—with our soul.

Our soul takes inventory and archives our progress throughout the journey of our lives through feelings and the love we have felt—

not from what you do or have in your possession. Our souls do not register how many cars we own or how big our houses are, or how many relationships we have had. It *does* care about the home in your own heart, if you are comfortable with your self, or if you have loved and allowed love. It registers the sum total of your experiences and how this has affected your passage; how you steered your awareness into the ocean of living consciousness.

If we continue to chase the dragon's tail, however, from this to that, from him to her, from less to more, we offer the chance of running our lives on the treadmill that keeps us in the neo-slavery of survival mode. We offer the chance of missing the mark of the inner richness of our feelings that connects us to our heart and soul.

We must allow ourselves to go deeper into the caverns where our inner dragons dwell. We must take courage and take a stand with a strong backbone to witness the sensations and feelings from a stand-still point without latching onto the tail of the dragon.

ACTIVATION

Where in your life do you feel thrashed around, desperately trying to fix this or that? How often do you endeavor to change your external circumstances at the expense of your inner world of self-feeling and healing?

Let the dragon thrash its tail around as much as it wants in your mind, but remember to let go of the tail and allow yourself to sink down into the deeper cavern of your body to feel the sensations. Watch your emotions from a standstill point—from the witness point—and breathe. Once they are felt without judgment, the transformation and transmutation from shadow to light, from pain to pleasure, from relentless dragon to a gentle purry cat will become apparent.

Doubt:
The Forebearer
of Certainty

- Doubt in our emotional repertoire has a bad rap. Doubt need not be a tainted emotion, but helpful in us to reach further, to use the struggle and move through the resistance, which can propel us further in the direction we are heading.

Like the birthing process, where a baby has to make its journey inching forward, nudging through its narrow passage to make headway to the other side of resistance and into ease and comfort of their mother's loving arms, Doubt accompanies us through the struggle process. With the desire to succeed, we inch forward bit by bit through the narrow canal of discomfort, edging us forward toward the goal of relief.

If we didn't have to contend with it, we could very well miss out on the value that working toward our goals can bring. For how is a pearl created? It is through the resistance and constant irritation of the sand on the mollusk over time that the lustrous pearl is developed. The ongoing irritation is the very impetus that creates such a worthy gem, which gives it the worthiness of fame. If we did not have to contend with doubt in our lives, we may just fall into lackadaisical complacency. We may not find the value or self-worth that is gleaned over time as we develop our emotional muscles to inch through the darkness, the unknown, the resistance and fear. The inner pearl—the wisdom—may just remain hidden under the ocean's sands of time.

Doubt is the forbearer of certainty, giving delineation and structure through the contrast of its shadow to the light. Everything as we know it has its polar opposites: The south and north pole keep the polarity of Earth in check; birth and death keep the stream of humility balanced; and Spirit and Matter dance the interplay of manifestation, to name a few. In the world of polarity, doubt, which produces a feeling of heaviness and unease in the body, holds lightness and ease at the other end of its potential. For how can we know lightness without heaviness, or ease without unease? How can we know certainty without the contrasting element of doubt? We need not shun it or run from it, lest we get stuck in the canal of fear. The irritations and aggravations are the elements that, after all, create the gem of wisdom that awaits us.

When you next feel doubt creeping in, focus on where you are heading at the end of the tunnel—the outcome. Be gracious that you are carving a path and making headway into the light of day.

Doubt is not something to be afraid of, nor should it be feared that it will hold you back. Rather, let it edge and urge you along the passage of which ease and grace await. Doubt has great value and merit in building a deeper sense of clarity—and both doubt and certitude work hand in hand, together as a team in the advancement toward your progress.

ACTIVATION

Where are you stuck in the passage of doubt? Relax and let go of the struggle. Let it know that it is welcome as part of the journey toward certainty and clarity, and that it is the other side of the coin of confidence. Set your sight on the positive outcome and know that it awaits at the end of the struggle.

Desperation is the
Mother of Transmutation

Desperation fuels the fire for change and beyond. Likewise, the first section of a rocket, known as a step rocket, is needed for launching and propelling the spacecraft into orbit. But once it has reached a certain level of momentum it is jettisoned, as it has done its job and is no longer required.

The surge for needed change and motivation is much the same in our own lives. It seems that we too often require a propellant, such as desperation, to fuel our own engine in order to launch us to higher ground. Desperation is not a dirty word. It holds great capacity and power to take you to that brink of no return, to first send you down to the stone-cold floor on your knees, to the rock-bottom place within where there is nowhere else to turn. It is there where we are humbly placed at the starting point of learning to stand on our own and walk again. At the depths, we have nowhere else to turn but to look upward and lift our heads to the heavens and ask for the grace of God to show us the way and to laugh and love again.

It is not that we must *rely* on desperation to be the impetus for corrective change. We can also use our focus, our confidence, and discipline along each step of the way to propel us to higher ground. The ego and negatory mind, however, would often have its way to make us play a smaller role in life to "keep us safe" from uncertainty and the unknown. We have all reached this place within ourselves, where we drop to our knees either literally or figuratively at one time or another. It is a reset of sorts, a clearing of the old, and a resurgence into the new.

Desperation builds the energy in the crucible of your being and gathers the impetus to create alchemical change. A reworking takes place that is so powerful that it transmutes us from the death of the old into the birth of the new, from burden to ease, from fear to courage, and from density to levity.

Desperation is like the firebird known as the phoenix that crashes to the ground in its own dying ashes before it resurrects to the heights of its new flight. It unleashes the repressed fire of imprisoned emotional energy trapped in the solar plexus, creating a cauldron to burn away the old that can no longer continue to coexist with life.

Like the mother of all change, Desperation gives birth to the exalted self—the one that is no longer contracted by fear—which can create a burst of change free from worry of how it looks as it has already seen (and been seen) at its worst... Nowhere else to go but upward and outward!

Like the rocket and the phoenix bird that are propelled into these unseen heights, we can use desperation as the fuel toward our mission accomplished. So, no, desperation is not something we should judge and avoid; rather, we can use its medicine to heal us in ways we have not known before, remembering that Desperation is the Mother of Transmutation.

ACTIVATION

The next time you find yourself humbly on your knees, where you have reached the rock-bottom place, remember that there is nowhere else to go but to look up. Allow the burning fuel of desire for change to propel you upward and forward.

What Comes Up,
Comes Out

• How and when did we learn to suppress what our bodies are
  releasing, and what and when our feelings will be expressed?
  We swallow our sputum when the body has invested time
  and energy to sweep it out from the deeper interiors of the
lungs. We conceal a pimple with medicated cream that suppresses
the skin's attempt to release impurities and drives toxic waste deeper
into the body to be reprocessed all over again. Most of us run to the
doctor to get a "quick fix" to block the pain without taking a moment
to discover what the body is attempting to tell or ask of us. Our
propensity is to push down and hide what the body naturally wants
to bring up and then out.

Bodily symptoms such as aches and pains, exudations and dis-
charges, lumps and bumps, are the only way the body can communicate with us, what it is undergoing and what it needs from us.
Humans seem to show more attentiveness to their cars' needs when
something rattles or shakes, than their own bodies!

We have all experienced one time or another when a toddler tugs
on our clothes for our attention, or for just a moment of our time, so
we can look at the child to see what it needs. Our bodies also tug on
us when they need our attention, expressing themselves in their own
language through bodily symptoms, aches and pain. This is how the
body communicates with us that something is not quite right and
that it might be needing something from us. Like a child, when we

ignore it or tell it to be quiet and attempt to silence it, it tugs at us more assertively and can eventually get loud and demanding, eventuating in a tantrum of sorts in order to be heard.

When neglected, bodily symptoms become compacted until they become longer-standing chronic situations that will eventually demand even more attention and time to recover and restore good health. The body, in all its brilliance, knows exactly what to do and how to behave—in other words, to "be-and have" of itself. It knows how to keep itself in check as a self-regulatory system through the process known as "homeostasis," of keeping a stable balance between the interdependent organs and elements of the body. If we would only let it do its job without our interference, without our attempt to ignore or hide what it is trying to tell us, we could create more of a balance between the body and mind! When we take more time to listen to its wisdom and follow its genius, it will help us align to a more correct pathway to our wellness, and we could lead more fulfilling lives all around.

The same equation applies to our emotions. From an early age, most of us have been taught to "behave and be a good child." We are told to be seen and not heard, to "keep a zip on it," "do not get angry, do not scream, do not be a crybaby, do not express your passion or natural sexuality and definitely do not speak your truth!" It is no wonder we suppress our feelings, gulp down our sorrow, swallow our authentic truth and hold back our tears. We wipe away and try to suppress our tears from streaming down our faces as if it is a shameful act to cry. Crying is one of the most natural of our bodily responses that is said to offer positive health benefits. So when our eyes cry, it is the body's attempt to release the emotional build-up of longstanding tension by excreting stress-inducing hormones. How brilliant is that?

If we allow the body to do what it knows best to do, to allow its natural flow of organic processing, we would all be in a more balanced emotional condition as a whole. Yet, somewhere along the way, we were told that bodies are shameful and that something is wrong when uncomfortable feelings arise. We'll practically do anything to circumnavigate those uncomfortable sensations of the body.

We'll take medications and drugs, distract ourselves with chatter, watch movies, get really busy, buy new clothes, a new car—anything to not feel what is actually going on in the present and unfolding moment. Over the years we begin to normalize such suppression and become separate from our own inner biorhythms and more importantly, lose respect for our human self.

In the natural human act of sexuality as well, we tend to stop breathing and hold back our passion as if it is unacceptable to relax, release and let go into the intimacy. We need to *let go...*

Let the body, let God, let what comes up come out!

Mother Nature again shows us how to do it and be it; she shows us how the seed grows up and out, from the dark soil into the light. Mother Nature doesn't suppress anything, she is constantly expressing, creating, letting go, revealing what comes up from her innermost self.

As we continue to hold back and suppress our natural feelings, our bodies become overloaded with emotional burdens that have been driven and pushed down deeper in the tissues and muscle memory. Something sooner or later has to give. The pipe will leak and, with continuing pressure, will burst. Our feelings and emotions need an outlet lest they get stuck and become energetic blockages that are driven into the deeper strata of the body and eventually manifest as ailments we call dis-ease. Imagine if we kept eating, swallowing more and more food, and didn't release what our bodies need to let go of! Chronic constipation would ensue, causing a blockage in the colon, in our own pipe-works, where toxic waste would surmount to the point of actually poisoning us.

Like a bubble of water that rises to the surface to be released into thin air, so too must we let the body do its appointed job and offer it up into open space. We need to let it be seen and recognized for what it is attempting to communicate to us—to let what comes up, come out—to let it go into the grace of life's simple act of living. Remember, once released, our bodily tensions, toxins and blocked emotional energy will be cleared, creating more space for the goodness that life wants to give.

ACTIVATION

Grant yourself permission to experience the uncomfortable feelings as they arise from the darker recesses of your being, like the bubble of water rising to the surface, to let them come up and out and into the light of awareness. Do not abandon, reject, or shame yourself but rather, have a communicative experience with your body by tending to its needs, and listen to your body as if it is the most intimate friend or companion you have. Ask your body questions. "What are you trying to say to me? What do you need? How best can I help you?" Trust in the first answer that arises, as it is usually the most correct one before the mind interjects and doubt sets in.

Since our feelings are felt in the body, ask the same questions to your sensitive feeling self, to your inner child that may need your attention and acceptance. How would you speak to a small child that is frightened, sad, or feeling abandoned or rejected at that moment? What would that child need to hear and feel from you in order to feel safe and accepted? Being gentle, being present and reassuring can assure this inner sensitive part of self that it is not alone and that everything is going to be okay, and that you are there with it every step along the way. Embracing it in the moment of its murmur before it has to scream for your attention will create more trust within the entirety of self.

Heart as Center

One might ask, "What is 'centering myself' and where is my center?"

When we refer to ourselves, we automatically place our hand over our heart, like an instinctive and inherent knowing that the center of our true being—of our conscience—is right there at our heart. We also know that when we refer to the heart of something, we are relating to the center of that thing, place, organization or family.

Many of us are not fully aware of the varying dimensions of the heart as our center as there are different levels that we can be cognizant of in fully appreciating and experiencing the heart. We can relate and connect to the heart on the physical, the esoteric/spiritual, and the healing heart level.

The Physical Heart:

The physical heart is regarded as the most vital organ which keeps us alive. It is a staunch and perpetual pump that circulates blood, vital in sustaining life, to every cell in the body. With every breath we take and each heartbeat, fresh oxygenated blood is circulated and delivered throughout the body. The body uptakes the fresh blood and transports the oxygen-depleted blood to the heart, which pumps it to the lungs to be released through the exhale. This process happens with every heartbeat, which is said to beat one hundred thousand times a day, up to forty million times a year and up to three billion times in an average lifespan.

The science of HeartMath affirms that the physical heart acts as a generator that creates a coherent and stable resonance within the body. This can influence the brain to experience increased health benefits, with greater mental and intuitive ability. (www.heartmath.com.)

Gregg Braden, a renowned pioneer in the emerging paradigm of science, social policy and human potential, in one of his keynote speeches on HeartMath in New Mexico, U.S.A., spoke of how the heart cognizes and responds neurologically and compassionately to an ailing tree before we actually see the tree itself! He qualified this by informing us that it holds a very powerful electromagnetic field; in fact, 5,000 times more powerful than the brain. Containing 40,000 neurons, the heart can act as our feeling brain—a brain of empathy and compassion. (Gregg Braden, "Gregg Braden on Heart Brain—Coherence, Global Awakening & Evolution of Consciousness," YouTube, GreggBraden.com, February 13, 2021, www.youtube.com /watch?v=3KEv-oQe0jI.)

This electromagnetic current is extremely powerful in creating and manifesting the coherent field of love and compassion that speaks volumes beyond the words of the mind.

As a congruous complement to the brain, the heart also helps to keep our emotional balance in check by inhibiting stress through the release of the hormone oxytocin—often called the "love hormone"— that can help promote trust, empathy, and bonding in relationships. This allows us to make better choice-making decisions for ourselves, our families, and our planet.

The Esoteric Heart:

Starting with the chakra system in the body, it is important to know that chakras are not physical, but rather centers or wheels of light that transmit and receive energy and information. The yogi masters of the Hindu tradition have brought to light that there are seven chakras that run along the center channel in line with our spine of which each correlate to one of the seven endocrine (hormonal) glands in the body. Each holds a stream of expertise that governs and maintains an energetic balance in that area.

The heart chakra lies at the midpoint of the chakra stream between the three upper chakras of the throat, third eye and crown chakras, and the three lower chakras of the root, sacral and solar plexus chakras. It is situated at the midpoint between the more spiritual nature and the physical nature of our beings; the bridge between the Above and Below/Heaven and Earth.

The esoteric heart does not duel for one side or another to win or to judge one thing over the other as the mind does. Instead, it works to integrate the opposites and embrace them as one whole. It is the *great balancer* that returns us to a place of compassion, love, and forgiveness, into a unified field rather than to generate separation.

The heart center is at the helm of our body vehicle. It is the compass that steers us back into alignment when we stray from our direct truth. It not only points us to our inner truth, but also to the True North, in vertical alignment and grounded with Earth and Heaven, in line with the Divine, keeping us close to the throne of God and in sacred balance. As our own built-in GPS system steers us toward our inner truth, we could take more trust and courage to follow its lead.

Our heart can also be considered as our own inner drum that beats at a steady rhythm to keep us synchronized with Mother Earth's natural heartbeat. Its pulse vibrates at the frequency of 7.83 Hz, also known as the Schumann Resonance, and emits an alpha/theta brainwave frequency in the human brain. It is this frequency that creates a relaxed, almost sleep state in which cell regeneration and healing can happen. Much like our own heart, Mother Earth's heart resonance enables regeneration and circulation of Life Force for the enlivenment not only for humanity but for all living things.

The heart chakra, as a transmitter and receiver of Universal Life Force, is the center from which the greater impulse of pure Love pours in from Source Energy direct. It is a wormhole to our inner dimensions, to our inner space. We could relate it as our own reset button, the zero point of singularity that allows us to refresh our physical, emotional, and mental selves. It is our own inner vortex that we can sit in at the center of, as the spin and the craziness of the world surrounds us. It is a place where nothingness and everythingness coexist, where the dance of light and darkness pulsate, from that which brings forth manifestation and dissolution of Matter and Spirit.

Our heart center is our home place within, to our authentic and pure selves. If we gave it more of our attention and respect for the truly amazing gift it is, we would fall in love with ourselves.

The Healing Heart:

The heart center is the hub from which we feel the expansion of love, the depth of compassion and the surrender of forgiveness. We do not feel such things in our elbows, or our toes or our legs; we feel it right there at the center of our being.

We feel the immensity and totality of our experience—whether painful or pleasurable—in our heart. It is understandable that we instinctively shield or even close our hearts to protect them from hurt and pain. Our deeper and inner work is to clear those blockages, heal the pain and forgivingly set down the armor to allow the heart to breathe, to do what it does best to point us to our inner truth, to shine love and be able to receive love more readily.

We can truly hear the subtle voice of the innate wisdom of our hearts once we quieten our thoughts to clear the static of the mind. Opposing thoughts create doubt and confusion, clouding our clarity and the ability to tune in. It is the "first inkling"; the "first thought" from the pure space of our hearts that arises before the mind has a chance to doubt it, which is the one we need to follow. We have gotten way too busy and hectic in our lives and have forsaken the one place that gives us refuge from the madness of the outside world— our Heart. This center is our safe space, our private sector where no one can interfere or interrupt our inner peace. As we bring more conscious awareness to breathe into, listen to the wisdom and have a conversation with our heart, we would know more clearly the "right" and resonant choices that can reverberate goodness in our lives.

The Light of God, of Source Energy, shines its light equally and eternally to all of us inclusively, as does the light of the sun. Yes, there are clouds that shield its light from us and we may say that the sun is not out today—but it is. It always is, no matter what.

Our protective armory and shields that cover the light of our hearts can also seem as though the light of love (and of life) has diminished or left us. But it has not. We need to make it a priority to clear the looming clouds of darkness that are impeding the light to shine to and from our heart. We need to be willing to feel all that we have suppressed and hidden from ourselves and from the light of the world. For that is the way to soften the hard shell and shield we have placed over our heart. We can forgive, have compassion for our hurts and pain, and love ourselves with full regard.

ACTIVATION

Are you willing to take some deep breaths to clear those clouds away? To feel and release the sorrow and pain so that it does not conceal the sacred altar of your heart?

Are you willing to breathe in the love that is always there for you, just like the sun, to release the notion and investment that you are alone and separate in your hurt and pain?

Give it the time it deserves. Listen to what your heart needs and respond in kind. Give gratitude to the compassion and love it eternally provides.

Becoming an
Antenna of Light

Just as the trunk of the tree is the conduit from which nutrients, sunlight and rain move back and forth from roots to leaves, our spine, too, is the column from which Light and Spirit (living force energy) move back and forth between Earth and Heaven. This column of light is a stairwell of consciousness; a conduit that passages living force energy back and forth from root to crown chakra, from Matter to Spirit and from Human to the Divine. Ever reaching its higher zenith, evolution moves upward, outward, and onward.

The body's nervous system illustrates this perpetual impetus and drive toward evolution by means of an Action Potential. It sends a voltage of electrical energy across the nerves and neural network, which instigates the release of neurotransmitters (chemical messengers) that make the quantum leap across the synaptic cleft (nerve junctions) to either excite, inhibit or modulate a nerve, in order to potentiate an action in the body. Ensuring optimum transmission of energy, it works in constant motion toward the driving force of evolution, to the next level of altitude and amplitude. As such, evolution in motion breaches the spectrum of restriction beyond the scope of thoughts and beliefs, releasing us from the bonds of limitation.

The physical spine, along with the energetic spine of our chakra system, houses the inner column of light to activate our potential.

Together they become our Antenna of Light. They receive light-energy into our bodies and transmit it out as love into the universe. We are indeed magnificent life and light forms that are equipped with a self-regulatory mechanism to evolve beyond measure. Like neurons, we ourselves are ever driving our action potentials toward a progressive future.

It is a discredit to the human race that societal programming has steered us away from the alignment of our internal antenna that can receive and transmit the clarity of our own decisions. We are instead led to believe that we are not enough in ourselves and that we need to look outside of ourselves for validation and confirmation. We are taught that we require a teacher, a guide, a priest or a guru to show us the path to the Divine. From early religions, we have been shunned from going straight to Source-God but instead, we must go through a priest in order to connect with the Divine. We have now become accustomed to hand over our convictions and our strengths to our friends, family, and broader outside influences. Thus, we bend our antenna out of shape and lean it toward the horizontal plane toward "the other" for validation, approval, and acceptance instead of keeping it vertically aligned with our own inner column of light that we can calibrate from.

This has created a kink, leaving us standing crooked to our own devices, weakening the line of reception from the Divine and stooping from our erect-ability to stand strong in ourselves. Our innate connection to the Divine has become misaligned and skewed, our spines "out of whack," as the constant bending of our antennas promotes a deviation from a self-generating authority and sovereignty.

Our spine is not only imperative to the health of setting the precedence of communication from mind to body and from body to mind, but also represents our "backbone," our moral fiber and the uniformity of thought-and-action, of our inner state of being. When our morale collapses into the "not good enough—I am unworthy" syndrome that our societal programming perpetually affirms, it hinders the flow of energy that moves through this canal and stunts our growth. It impedes our natural evolution to connect and expand toward the light. We may feel thwarted and defeated, resulting in a spinal collapse; a stooping over into a lack of confidence, followed by a sense of depression.

Leaning into "the other" is a natural quality of being human—to touch, be touched, to communicate, to relate, to reflect—but we must remember not to hand over our own inner God-given authority, our own intuition or gut feeling, to others. Our emotional and spiritual self-reliance and self-empowerment starts at the inner corridor of integrity, of our spines.

How to adjust our antenna?

We are inspired to remember the vertical plane of our True North that is centered in the heavens above. We must stand with our strong trunks as trees on the Earth, with roots in the ground and yet reaching toward the light. From the Below to the Above, our spines will more likely stack up and stand erect like a tower of light to be more able to follow the line of pertinence to the Divine.

We are lighthouses, Antennas of Light! With erect and straight spines, our consciousness is more likely to flow more freely and receive the divine transmission available to each and every one of us. We have long evolved past the horizontal plane of existence and are now invited to remember to realign to the vertical plane of evolution, with our own free and natural ability to navigate the road to higher consciousness. We must remember that we need to listen to the transmission we receive from our own connection to the higher government of Source Energy direct.

Like the passage of nutrients that travel along the trunk of the tree, we stand with our spines upright, strong and erect, reaching for the light, reaching heavenwards for our spiritual sustenance and subsistence with our consciousness, progressively moving toward the highest reaches of possibility. As Antennas of Light, we receive the information of light and transmit the higher frequency of love along the path of evolution.

ACTIVATION

Stand firmly on the ground and sense into your spine and chakra pathway. Feel into the flow of energy to see if your antenna has any bends or kinks in it. Is it bent toward others, or does it stand strong and upright in its own might? If you sense, see or feel your antenna is out of alignment, re-adjust it back into its vertical axis to allow the free flow of energy and light along the road to your own positive evolution.

Chakras as the Stairwell to Higher Consciousness

The chakras of the body not only act as an Antenna of Light but also exemplify the perfect stairwell to higher consciousness. There are seven main chakras serving as stations of energy that are situated vertically from the base of the spine to the top of the head. Even though they are not physical in form and structure, they are highly energized centers or wheels of light that serve as a conduit for the reception and transmission of energy to our souls, the Universe and to each other. From ground to top floor, from root to crown chakra, from Earth to Sky, from Matter to Spirit, they rise from the Below to the Above to take us to the place of higher viewing and experiencing.

Beginning from the root chakra at the base of the spine, the energy is earth-oriented and signifies the mainstay and grounding of our energy. It is the base, the foundation at ground level from which the energy, like a plant, moves up the chakra stem with its roots in the ground and the eventual flowering at the crown chakra toward the light.

The renowned saying and sage wisdom from the Eastern Hindu philosophy "from the cesspool grows the lotus" exactly depicts this ascension journey along the chakra stem. From the mire, the muck of swampy and boggy land grows the loftiest and holiest of flowers; a yogic and meditational symbol of higher consciousness and spirituality. From the mud of our own murky, unclear minds and the emotional vault where our shadows hide and lurk is where the energy and fuel, acting as fertilizer, drive us upward along our growth and spiritual consciousness.

Each chakra is depicted by a color and a certain number of lotus flower petals:

- Four petals at the base—*red*
- Six at the sacral center—*orange*
- Ten at the solar plexus—*yellow*
- Twelve at the heart chakra—*green*
- Sixteen petals at the throat chakra—*blue*
- Two petals at the third eye chakra—*indigo*
- One thousand petals fully opened and bloomed at the crown chakra—*violet*

As we move up the chakra stem, we see that more and more petals open to represent a higher or more attuned frequency of energy, opening to the Divine. The third eye chakra, however, harnesses the passage of dual energies that wind up from the root chakra, which is depicted by two petals, to signify the union of opposites that conjure and summon the blooming for a fully opened lotus flower at the crown center toward the heavens. This final opening at the very top of our heads, completing the bloom path, represents the "thousand-petaled lotus" at the crown chakra, our true crown of light that connects us to the celestial realms and of higher consciousness. A pure flowering arising out of a cesspool!

The polarity of root to crown and mud to lotus such as this is constantly demonstrated through the universality of dual forces such as Day and Night, Light and Shadow, Birth and Death, Truth and Falsity...to name just a few. From trials we are rewarded with tribulations, from death we are given the gift of life, from falsehood the truth is always revealed, from the silence sound emerges, from stillness there is movement. From the mud, the divine lotus grows!

Our compass points need to point to our True North. That is above each and every one of us, no matter where we are on the planet.

If our bodies stand in the vertical plane in the south, then our heads always point to the north. The polarity of the opposing forces once again holds the universal flow in balance. One pole could not possibly be more valid and divine than the other, for they each need the other to validate and balance each other in wholeness. If we could but stand at the fulcrum of polarities and regard each polarity as valid and divine as each other, we could rise above the "struggle of duality" and accept the fullness each brings to the equation.

The most pivotal chakra that can act as the fulcrum of polarities that helps to balance out the dualities of the chakras and of the mind's constant play is the heart chakra, which lies at the midpoint between the two chakra poles of the base and crown. It is situated between the three lower chakras of the base (root) chakra, the sacral chakra and the solar plexus, and the upper three chakras of the throat, the third eye chakra, and the crown chakra. Their collective energy, as seen through the spectrum of light, correlates to the same sequence as the rainbow refracting light through moisture.

The heart chakra is where our arms extend out to the world. It is where the lotus plant leaves balance the stem and extend out to receive the light of the sun and the love of Nature Divine. This chakra is the seat of the three-folded flames of Love, Compassion, and Forgiveness, acting as our truest sense of origin and source from which God's/Universal Love flows. The wisdom of choice that comes from the heart is always a non-biased choice—the balanced choice—from which acceptance of the whole is unified. For the heart knows not of judgment and separation but encompasses love and acceptance as its modus operandi. The mind is always ready to leap into the "this or the that"; the preferential bias that arises from the idea that one side is better than the other. The heart chakra, however, is all-inclusive, without judgment. It embraces the All That Is without the separation that judgment spawns.

It is important at this point to mention that not only is the fertilizer for growth based at the root chakra where the mud of consciousness lies, but our creative Life Force Energy as well. Many know of the word "kundalini," which is renowned and esteemed in the Hindu yoga world. Kundalini in the ancient Hindu language of Sanskrit connotes "she who is coiled," implying the feminine serpentine creative energy that lies at the base of the spine. We feel this energy on the verge of sexual climax; that energy that is unsurmountable; the surging force that rises from the base of the spine to the top of the head to dissolve us into the illumination of the higher realms. Moving along its path, like a serpent, it clears blockages and stuck energy as it makes its assent through the chakra stem to the crown chakra. Along this chakra stairwell to the Divine, it releases and clears away what has been stuck at the basement of our being, and rises to the occasion to be set free to the outreaches of Source existence.

Utilizing it consciously and wisely, kundalini energy affords us the ability to channel itself all the way from the darkness of the inner quagmires to the lightness and open space above—from the animal base to the evolved human.

It is not hard to see why old religious orthodox indoctrination would have us shun this aspect of our human sexuality unless used for procreation alone. It is a very powerful creative source of energy that we are summoned, time and time again, to be very respectful of its power and transformational impact in our lives. Creative Life Force Energy grants us the potential to co-create humanity, to utilize the momentum of manifestation, and to access the highest reaches of consciousness.

In equal value and merit, our physicality and sexuality (based at the root) and our spirituality (at the crown) illustrate once again the forces of polarity creating the one connected whole, like roots of the lotus in the mud giving rise to a fully opened lotus flower to the sky. We need not judge one over the other, but rather embrace them both as equally valid, necessary, and divine forces that complete the totality of our existence.

The heart chakra becomes the magnet for both polarities of our being. It is the place of full regard, the home place where acceptance and love await. Each and every one of us is blessed with a chakra stem—our own stairwell to higher consciousness from which our

True North points. Our chakra stem/system becomes a living staircase of light from which direct transmission occurs from Heaven to Earth and Earth to Heaven. Thus, it creates the perfect stairwell to higher consciousness.

ACTIVATION

The following exercise helps to clear stuck energy through the chakra stem and through the root chakra into the earth to allow for a clear passage of transmission and reception of energy from both Earth and Sky energies. It also allows additional space for you to think more clearly, become more present, and focus and function more effectively through your busy day.

You can also use it to channel the light of the sun and of the Universe into your body and usher it down as it cleanses and nourishes the entirety of your being.

Sitting on the ground (indoors or outdoors) or on a chair, on a pillow or on your bed, lift your shoulders up and back in a relaxed way with your head straight forward (not bent up or down) to allow the energy to flow freely up and down the chakra stem. Take a nice, deep breath in through the nose and exhale and let go from the mouth, finding a steady flow, continuing to breathe this way, in through the nose and out of the mouth.

After a few breaths on the next exhale, become the breath and follow it with your awareness, taking with it the excess and mental static from your head, all the way down your central lane, your chakra stem, until it eventually lands into the root chakra.

Continue breathing in through the nose and out from the mouth. Allow each exhale to find its way and sink down and settle with the gravity of the Earth, into that stable and steady place at the base of your being.

After a few breaths or when you feel ready, contract and release the perineum (between the anus and the genitals) a few times and relax, and let go of the release. Then on the next exhale, allow the breath—the energy—to come in and down and follow it through the root chakra and down into the Earth, and LET GO, RELEASE and SURRENDER anything that has been held in or stuck, and free it into Mother Earth like the dead leaves of a tree for her to recycle and repurpose this energy as fertilizer for your growth and nourishment.

Breathe into this feeling of letting go, of surrender and peace. Take note of how it feels to let go, surrender and ground your mental energy into the loving arms of Mother Earth.

—From Amalia's shamanic teaching course: "*Stronger Than Ever*" found on her website www.earthspiritwisdom.com.

The Heart Chakra at the Hub of Our Being

Our chakra stem is often referred to as the "rainbow bridge" because it encompasses the spectrum of light from red to violet and follows the same suit of colors as the rainbow. The base chakra at the bottom of the chakra stem energetically correlates to the color red, as illustrated at the top of the rainbow. The crown chakra at the top of the chakra stem vibrates to the frequency of the color violet, as it is depicted at the lowest tier of the rainbow. The color green lies at the center in both our chakra stem and the rainbow, with the respective colors of yellow and orange below and blue and indigo above the heart chakra, completing the full spectrum of light.

The center point of the chakra stem—the heart chakra—has a significant role in holding both ends equally in place. Its sphere of action acts as a pivot point of reference to the entirety of the whole.

At the hub, the heart center holds a noteworthy position in its chief role to keep our sense of self intact and in balance on an energetic, emotional, and spiritual level. Pulsing with love and peace with every heartbeat, it beckons us to return home to ourselves in every moment. It is a home base from which we must return to, time and time again, from which we have strolled. It is a space to rest, take a pause, and reinstate our sanctity in the maze of distraction of the unsound world around us.

When we refer to our self in conversation, we naturally touch our heart—not our head, our arm, or our feet, *but right there to our heart*—as a reference of who we are, to the sovereign and fullest sense of self. It is this deeper sense of self at the helm of our being, where our heart steers us to the midheaven point of our soul, our greater GPS (our global positioning system) that navigates and re-routes us back home to ourselves within. It does not steer us wrongly once we learn how to listen and follow its lead. It is in constant calibration to course-correct us back into the truth of self—not of others, but of self—and will always steer us in our soul's flow for our highest good.

Our heart calls us back time and time again to the humble sim-plicity of our innate innocence. Each heartbeat is an earnest appeal for the dedication of life. It speaks to us, not in a worded language, but a wordless language and with simplicity, not complexity. Its simple utterances require our wholehearted attention in order to listen to its wordless voice speak. All too often, our thoughts drown out this subtle voice, and we are left to decipher the muffled utter-ances behind the noise of the mind. By returning to the heart at the hub of our being, we may tune into a bandwidth that has less elec-trical static to listen through so we can hear its wisdom.

Its sphere of action in its own benediction is of love, forgiveness, and compassion. It is often symbolized as the three-folded flame of the sacred heart, the sacred flame that keeps alight the eternal Light of God. The heart is a place of sanctity that silently awaits us to humbly kneel at the hearth of our own inner altar, where our prayers can be felt and heard in our most private sanctum.

Here, in this holy place, is where all of life's experiences and feel-ings can be embraced without judgment and separation. Its prime directive, after all, is to circulate life-giving blood and nutrients to fill the entirety of the well of our being. As a chamber of wholeness that embraces duality, it tends to the unification of universal oppos-ites of self within; of the yin and the yang, of the inner masculine and feminine, and of the great Below and the great Above. It is in this chakra where the marriage of opposites can take place, here at the throne of consciousness, where our inner queen and king sit in the unified field of wholeness and integrity.

It is in the heart of unification where we can witness life as it is without judgment, and with compassion as we embrace suffering. This opens our hearts to gratitude and appreciation, which is key to living our lives in the frequency of abundance and fullness.

As a great teacher that resides at the hub of our being, our heart guides us toward wholeness, making its appeal with every pulse to return us to our center. As students of this great teacher, we could assist in clearing and releasing the blocks and shields we have placed over the heart to allow love, forgiveness, and compassion to flow through.

ACTIVATION

Take a few deep breaths, inhaling in from the nose and exhaling with an intent of surrender from your mouth. Drop your attention from your head and allow your awareness to land gently into your heart like a light feather on a small velvet pillow. Notice how it feels to breathe into your heart and just let yourself be there with it.

What does it look like energetically? What color is the energy? What shape? What is it needing from you in this moment? Be courageous enough to see it as it is without trying to change anything about it or "get rid" of any discomfort that may arise.

Embrace the feelings you have stored right there behind the shield of protection. Accept any feelings of not being good enough, not loved enough, the fear of judgment and disapproval, of doubt, and allow the notion of compassion to soothe and embalm your heart. Be compassionate and forgiving of yourself for attracting and creating the things that have "happened" to you. Have a gentle dialogue with it, and ask it questions as you let the answers arise directly from your heart.

As we learn to listen to the silent language of the heart, we will come to know that we can trust in our heart as a navigational guiding system in life and in our relationships.

The Gift of Giving

- Next time you are giving to someone, notice where that "giving" is coming from. Consider whether it is coming from an abundant overflow from your heart or a place of lack deep inside that is calling for your attention. Is there a lure dangling from the end of the line that you have cast so far outside of yourself? What are you are fishing for? Does your self-worth depend on how others receive it or what response they demonstrate?

If this act of giving—whether it be a gift, a donation, or an action—stems from a hidden place where neediness and lack reside, the repercussion of deficit will ensue. The act of giving from scarcity can leave you feeling deficient and empty, followed by the need to fill that feeling of emptiness of the void within. This magnifies the sense of insufficiency, which further fosters the need to seek an external source of fulfillment. This cycle thus creates a ceaseless loop of giving from the place of lack that continues to seek validation and approval. This casting out of your line to fish for consent and ratification may give you a fleeting sense of security, but continues to authorize your sense of deprivation.

Giving from an overflow of love, from genuine gratitude and abundance, will result in a fulfillment that is not contingent on whether you get something back in that moment or from that particular person.

Let us look at the phenomenon of tithing or donating to a cause. Notice if your "giving" derives from guilt that you "should" give or else you may not be *given to* at a time of your genuine need, or if it is about looking good in the eyes of others. The source of this energy is amplified and feeds the belief of guilt and lack.

To give from a place of generosity, from your loving spirit, no matter how much you give with no strings attached, astonishingly creates a path of abundance that flows back to you. Our ego has already determined that the more you give, the less you are left with, but your heart does not quantify the expression of love in this way. It knows that the more you give from this place of love and abundance, the more it is returned in a myriad of ways, unexpected and unfathomed.

Giving from the seed of this true giving acknowledges your abundance and gratitude for all that you receive and share from the richness of your spirit. This is where "Good Karma,"—your bank of goodwill—creates a positive feedback loop that spans throughout time and space and lifetimes, propagating true goodwill for self and others in kind.

This is a truth that many of us are far from understanding as a generative whole. If we shift the dial of intention and perception from lack to abundance, we can open to the unlimited treasures that await.

ACTIVATION

The next time you offer something or do a good deed for someone, take a moment to see where the impetus of that giving is coming from. Is it coming from a place of lack where you may expect an outcome for your own personal need, or is it stemming from an abundant overflow that is set free once you have given it?

Realationships

A relationship is literally and metaphorically, a "relationship"—a vessel of which we navigate and passage through
the ebbs and flows and the changing tides of the seas of our
relations with others.

There are varying waters and tidal flows we can encounter in
our relationships. Some are as placid as a lake, some are as rough as
a stormy sea, some cascade like waterfalls and others trickle along
like a bubbling brook.

Some relationships operate on a surface level, wading and splashing in the shallow waters, where it is safe with little or no risk.
Others can take you further into the depths of the ocean, where the
underlying currents run deep and where more challenges to stay the
course arise.

Wading in shallow waters doesn't connote that it is not or cannot be a "real" relationship, or that you are not committed to the
connection you share. It may not, however, reveal the stronger current between you that often depends on each other to reach the
tempered shoreline after the struggles that arise. For it is in deeper
waters where more weighty emotions lurk, that can bubble up to the
surface to bring up and out the real and more relative (relational)
dynamics between you. For the deeper the dive, the more intimacy
is experienced and the more that can be revealed in the process. This

type of relationship that calls for a deeper commitment and dynamic, I call a "*real*ationship."

Let us explore some of the more prevalent *real*ationships that we may passage through in our lives.

With God/Creator:

The tribal aspect of our humanness throughout time is that we have depended on one another for protection, survival, socio-economical and educational advancement. We have shifted from a tribal format to a nuclear family unit and more and more into our individual sovereignty for our sense of survival in a very complex societal network. The reorientation from the use of spears and arrows for hunting, living in caves and the subsistence of living has shifted into the making of a society where the majority have a choice of comfort and convenience readily available at every turn.

We are now at a point in our evolution where the majority have the option to control their indoor climate with a switch, go about their daily lives in relative safety, access provisions from a store and choose from a myriad of options to better themselves in staying the course. With less time needed to meet survival challenges, we have more time to reach into the higher realms of self within the container of prevailing comfort. We are at a time where we can reflect, ponder and expand our spiritual parameters to touch into something greater than what we ordinarily experience.

We have been programmed through the constant barrage of media, education, laws and regulations to be boxed within the parameter of fear and separation. Each and every one of us is corralled into the restricted confines of the inner prisons of our minds to believe we are limited, helpless, and most importantly, separate from the infinite capacity of God-Universe-Spirit. We have bought into the lie of the separation from Source of which we are birthed from.

We have yet to tap into the vastness and magnificence of the inner potential we can access; to throw our anchor into the deep ocean of existence and tether ourselves to a greater passage, to our greater body, to the All That Is. We have lived in a dream that has perpetuated a falsity that we need "the other" to become whole and complete. We are addicted to looking outside of ourselves for validation from all that surrounds us. Right there within is where we can take that deeper dive into the greater ocean to let go and surrender the regulations and the stipulations of the how's and what's and why's.

We need to allow the anchor of awareness within the tide of love's embrace to ground and tether us to something more secure within the Self. For in truth, we have all that we need within ourselves if we would turn our drifting eyes to the secure connection with our primary *realationship* to the Source of our creation—to God-Universe-Spirit.

By letting go and emptying our vessels from sabotaging thoughts that separation from Source can summon, we can more freely flow along the sea of life with more ease and grace, even when the churning currents and humongous waves of life challenge us. As we empty our cups to allow the flow of love and light to fill us, we find that we are not alone, but in direct relationship with something greater that is constantly flowing in.

This deepened connection with Self and God-Creator invites you to question limiting beliefs and to make a deeper inquiry into the nature of existence beyond the limited and mechanical mind. It can introduce you to the infinite horizon within the ocean of energy that you are a particle of.

With Ourselves:

We scramble on the rubble of lack and expect the other to hold us in high esteem. All aspects of our lives—our work, our relationships, our prosperity and our health—reflect to us our inner stance and stature. Each and every one of us is at the helm of our "ship" in our ocean's passage, and everything we see and experience is a reflection of our own inner universe of how we think and feel about ourselves.

We have, instead, displaced the importance of our fundamental relationship with our Whole Self and have cast the line so far away and out to sea. Without accepting and loving ourselves unconditionally, we can project the parts of us that we deem unlovable outwardly and expect others to love us no matter what. We often expect the other to be a lifebuoy for us when we feel like we are drowning and the pressures of life are dragging us down in the engulfing currents, when the other is endeavoring to stay afloat.

Of course, we help and give each other a helping hand, as to give and receive is part of our human nature. However, what if we could each stay buoyant with our thoughts and take more time for self-care, take the time to release and empty the heavy weight within that drags us down, be kinder to ourselves, learn to love ourselves, breathe, let go, shake it out, or take a walk in nature so that we may come to an even keel within? What if we opened ourselves like a chalice to be filled by the Light of Spirit, by the benevolent force of the Universe, by the love of God? Then we may be able to give more freely without conditions and from a whole and loving place within.

We are each responsible for filling our own cups directly from the grace of God, to take the time to steep and drink this loving stream and share the abundant overflow with others. We thus become a natural wellspring for others in need, especially those who have not yet reeled their line back into self.

With Others:

Let us start with the relationships between men and women as a working template for relating to "the other."

How can we have a real relationship between a man and a woman based on the misleading premise that we are opposite sexes?

As opposites, this infers that we are in *opposition* with each other as contestants in a competition, resulting in either a loser or a winner. If we adjust this perspective to see that we are complimentary to one another, rather than the opposite of each other, our course is corrected toward a brighter destination.

The arduous struggle between men and women as "opposite components" has left us wounded on the battleground in a war-torn territory. I call our attention, particularly to the patriarchal push for power we have witnessed throughout the ages of the control over the feminine gender: the agenda to own, dominate, constrain, mistreat and exploit her.

Many titles and terms contain a fixation of masculine overtones as an identification of the whole species. Words such as hu*man*, *his*tory, hu*man*ity and *man*kind all illustrate this bias toward the assumption that men are the more prominent and more significant sex. We can instead bring consciousness to unifying the dualistic differentiation between the sexes and start using the terms: *our*story instead of history, *our*kind instead of mankind, hu*formity* instead of humanity and hu*being* instead of human.

Ancient times, however, did substantiate the feminine and her intrinsic power through the worship of the Goddess and Mother Earth. Honoring the cycles of seasons, revealing the changing faces of the feminine and the bounty of harvest that she brings, has been honored and venerated for thousands of years. The feminine reign constituted power through the lineages of family, the temples and royalty. It was at the advent of organized religion when the Mother Goddess was desecrated and stomped upon to leave her far behind in the human recesses of history. The Goddess temples were desecrated and then built upon, burying the face of the Divine Feminine under the newly built churches that made the Father, Son, and the Holy Ghost the prominent spiritual advocates of the day.

In our most recent history, however, women were asked to step out from the stove and hearth and out of the shadows during the First and Second World Wars. Men away at war gave rise to many empty positions in the workplace and women were asked to fill in the void. Women were now becoming postmen, milkmen, factory workers, medical staff and physical laborers. This afforded women an increase in "her status" in both the workplace and in society, granting them a new sense of sovereignty over their financial welfare and increasing confidence. The control and ownership over women began to wane as women became able to support themselves. The push-back into the front line created the advent of feminism, of burning bras and shoulder pads and the movement for equality in the workplace. But this swing of power toward the feminine continued to feed the competition between men and women.

Now is the time to find even ground—no longer a battleground but a common ground—that honors the complementary contribution of both as equally valid and divine. We need to strengthen the co-valence bond between us with honor and respect for what and how we each bring to the equation.

Remember how we played with each other as toddlers, in the sandpit or the garden? Remember when you were curious about the sand, in wonder about the other child next to you? How others played with the sand differently than you, accepting with an open state of mind the differences we each had? Whether boy or girl, it didn't matter at that stage. We were all playing in the sandpit, in the garden, as equal players without conceptions or deceptions. In innocence and openness, we were free to experience the moment as it was, without wanting to change or manipulate the outcome.

We are not here in truth to blame, shame, or defame one another or even step over one another to get to the top, or to be right and make the win—no matter what type of relationship you share with another. Let us not waste precious time pulling each other down to clamber to the top with a smug smile, or belittle each other with downcast looks or hold judgment against our loved ones. There is a strong, addictive propensity to project our thoughts onto one another, which creates a codependency rather than a healthy bond with each other.

By respecting the complementary roles we each play in navigating through the ebbs and flows, the storms and calm seas of our relationships, we can help balance the mast and keep each other sailing on an even keel.

Let's change the lens of how we view and experience our relationships and shift the vantage point to become the captain at the helm of our own ship as we voyage through the ocean of life together.

ACTIVATION

How can you be kinder to yourself and give yourself the gift of letting go of the heavy weights that plummet you down into the bottom of the ocean? Who are you when you are connecting with the greater part of yourself in the ocean of life? What course-correction needs to be made to sail smoothly in your realationships?

Take a step back and really see "the other" as they are without judgment or projecting your fears upon them.

Delving into this inner inquiry can enrich and widen the lens of which you experience the Universe, Self and Others.

Slowing Down

Have you noticed that when someone slows down in the way they talk, walk, and move that they magnetically draw your attention closer to them? You are pulled into their deeper interior where you can hear, sense, and feel more clearly what they are expressing. Somehow, the energy and field around them feels more tangible and palpable when their inner and outer space is not filled with fragmented thoughts and agitated movement.

The next time you are watching a slow-motion segment in a movie, notice how much more you can capture of the details that you may otherwise miss. Movie directors use slow motion when they wish to enhance a scene, to capture our focus and attention, and create suspense—which encourages the viewer to pay closer attention to what is going on. The frames are stretched, which enhances the *emotion* that is being inferred or expressed, giving us a fuller experience rather than fragmented moments in time. Everyone and everything look more beautiful, like poetry in motion, giving us the notion that we actually experience the feeling ourselves in suspended grace.

In contrast, the fast-forward motion or fast-paced action segments do not afford us the time to capture details, nor does it allow us to step into the feeling of the scene. Even though there is a purpose in speeding up the motion to incite thrill and excitement, we are "seeing" it with the critical time sense of edginess rather than "experiencing" the roundness of it.

The rapid pace of our lives today can exceed our natural ability to experience our selves and others with ease and calm. Our movements have become fast-framed, harder and sharper, separating our moment-to-moment movements into a series of images and fragmented slivers of reality. When we are rushing, hurrying, and scurrying to "get things done," our day becomes filled with freeze-framed, separated moments of time. We become regimented soldiers marching into the orders of the day to get the next item on the list done. We have become neo-slaves of our own doing.

This holds the nervous system hostage to stress, to soldier on, to survive rather than to thrive in the experience of truly living. Our nervous systems need time to assimilate and regulate the influx of stimuli that is coming in from all directions. We need time to calibrate and to feel our experience in any given moment in order to make the best decisions for ourselves and live a more fulfilled life. Pushing forward, striving toward, talking faster, and fitting as much as we can into our day robs us of living in the *now moment*, which never operates with a sense of hurry. In this fraudulent way of living, of cutting corners, we rob ourselves and others from the truth of our experience.

Slowing down lessens the agitation and smoothens the sharp edges of our lives. The wheel of life in the natural world is rounded in its energy, and the chemistry of its organic compounds is circular in composition. When we ourselves move a little slower with less agitation in our movement, we can feel ourselves moving through our lives in a smoothened sense and with a more natural glide throughout the day. We are more able to elongate the tempo of the day with a slower, more assimilable sine wave rather than an angulated spike wave, to notice the details of what we may need to address at any given moment.

Whales are great teachers of how to move in this slower sine wave motion. They show us how to move smoothly and glide through the waters with calm and ease. When a whale breaches out of the water or its tail waves in the air, the grace of its slow and rounded movement magnetizes you into the participation of its sensory experience.

The momentum of time is elongated so that you fall into its un-fathomable beauty. You almost become the whale. You are not seeing it, but feeling it.

The eagle, too, illustrates this ease and calm as it moves in slow, rounded wheels in the sky, drawing our full attention into its fight. Both the whale and the eagle, in their majesty of easeful grace, afford us the eternal memory of a moment unsurpassed.

The key to unraveling the complexity of our lives is in slowing down the tempo of our minds and our bodily movements enough to be in full cognizance of the experience we are having. When we slow down, we can move with the composure of self, pull into ourselves the respectful appreciation of others, and breathe more life and ease into our movements and actions.

If we can re-mind ourselves to slow down as we walk within our own homes and feel the flow of our energy throughout the space of our environs—to slow the pace of how we walk; to round out the edges of our strides and to breathe between our sentences—we may enjoy, with more fullness, the experience of life as it unfolds from one gliding moment to the next.

ACTIVATION

Remember the teachings of the whale and eagle in showing you how to stretch and elongate time by slowing down your pace. Slow down when chewing your food and when picking up your cup to drink. Walk in your own home more gracefully to enjoy your sur-roundings, create more grace-time between one appointment and the next to maintain your mental poise, and allow the frames of life to flow with more ease.

Walking meditation is a good training ground for slowing down both your mind and body. To begin, choose a place to walk with little or no distractions so you can fully focus on the sensa-tions of your feet and the ground on which you are stepping.

1. Pick up your foot and move it through space. Very gently and slowly, place it on the ground as you feel every sensation of each part of this process from heel to toe.

2. Walk with supreme intention and attention to reconnect with each living moment. Feel the body's weight and gravity of your feet in connection with the ground under you.

3. Walk in mindful meditation, with one foot after the other, as you focus and breathe along the way. If your thoughts take over, gently bring your attention and awareness back to the sensation of your feet and the slowing down of each step to ground your mind into the presence of your body.

THE SACRED WEAVE OF
EARTH SPIRIT WISDOM

Rocks are one of the most rudimentary expressions of Earth that exemplify the nature of existence. Their abidance of presence is a testament of time immemorial, which harbors a sanctum of silence that when met, can reveal the deep mysteries of living consciousness.

These ancient beings are the physical manifestation of silence that helps us remember our truest essence, re-instilling the knowing that we contain within us Mother Nature, God Nature. They represent the eternal force of boundless love that permeates our living experience; that part of us that can just be in the world of existence without having to prove ourselves to anything or anybody; that part of ourselves that knows we are good enough just as we are, and that can allow life to move through us like the changing seasons, currents, and tides of life.

Our emotional upheavals and exquisite experiences all come and go, while the rock-steady being within us remains eternally present.

We can call upon this part of our inner nature at any time to stand in our solidity, sit in our stillness, and breathe in the awareness of our rock-solid self. We can do this especially when sudden change may uproot our sense of sensibility and stability, when we are faced with adversity, or when we see certain aspects of our lives crumble around us. We can trust this grounded and most stable force within us that the rocks have attested to throughout the eons.

Earth herself is a stable force we can tap into. We can gather and harness all of our ideas, thoughts, and life experiences and root them into the ground of our being, into the presence of our being, just like the rocks and how the trees show us how to do. The mountains also summon their entirety in a collective form, undeterred by the momentum of change.

Within this stable force lies spirit beyond matter that suffuses all living and non-living things. The Universe is comprised of unlimited and boundless energy of the ether element we can call spirit. It is an energy which we do not see with our naked eyes but sense with all of our entirety.

Each living thing contains its own unique animated force; the elements, trees, plants, rocks, mountains, animals, people, stars, and planets hold their own essential quality. Each is an individualized expression of God—of the All That Is—and each is encoded with its own seed potential and sacred language. The Tree Spirit contains a wordless knowledge and the Rock Spirit has its own manner of communicating, and so on. As we attune ourselves to this sacred language, and learn how to listen to, comprehend and embody it, we begin to weave the threads of Wisdom of Earth and Spirit, thereby unifying the opposites into the entirety of Oneness.

Not only can we tap into this wisdom weave, but also shapeshift our energy into a tree to stand tall and strong, into a plant to grow toward the light, into a rock to embody the stillness, become as immovable as a mountain, or flow like the running waters and shine our light as brilliantly as the stars.

FINAL ACTIVATION

We can embody fully our EARTH selves:

Be and accept our full humanness to experience the bountiful realms of life that Mother Earth provides, and be grounded in our earth walk and fully present in our bodies.

We can expand and reach the heights of SPIRIT:

As we ground with the earth, we can elevate our thoughts, ideas, and intentions to connect with our spiritual and soul self.

We can fully embrace our WISDOM:

By becoming a divine bridge between Earth and Spirit, we can embody the sacred weave of our wisdom self.

We are bound by Earth and yet free by Spirit.
We are both human and spiritual, standing between the great above and the great below. We are sacred weavers within the great loom of living reality.

Together, we can weave the threads of
Earth and Spirit into the living testament of truth,
into the heart of ourselves, into the heart of Wisdom.

Tributes

To:

—Great Spirit, Mother Father God, Creator, Life and the principle of Love as the overarching benevolent principle that has guided me along the way, steering me toward the highest outcome for my life and for this book.

—Mother Earth that constantly abides in her beneficence of livingness and givingness, to all of her children. For the wisdom and counsel that she imparts to us freely at all times. You are the sanctity of life.

—Sedona, AZ for calling me to her so many years ago and for holding me close to her bosom and nest to allow me to grow my wings of confidence as a woman, healer, teacher, shaman priestess and author before spreading my wings to fly wide and far.

—My beloved family, mother Georgia, adopted father Manos and sister Nola in Australia who have always given me the good grace to follow my spirit and have never squelched my desire to be of service for the greater good at the expense of our proximity.

—My clients and students who have trusted me to guide and counsel them along their transformational path of healing body, mind and spirit. It is within my sessions with you that has inspired action and momentum to write this book. Thank you for extending and reaching new heights of your wisdom embodiment.

—The Awakened Press, Lindsay R. Allison Dierking, for seeing in full my potential, putting me under her wing and guiding me through the process from the beginning to the finish line, it has been a joy.

—My powerful guide that has been overarching with due diligence to ensure that everything from the beginning of the book to the end is placed correctly throughout the process.

—My beta testers: Hava Derby, Ed Benoit, Eric Lindemer, Barbara Bryan, Marla Schmidt, Angela Temple, Loren Lewisohn, Eddy Baccini, Charles Panzarella, Tajuana Thewlies, Dotty O Donnell, Terri Lee Fatouros, Sophie Shenton, Mary Fox and Steaven Brown, who read a portion of the excerpts and giving their honest feedback.

Finally:

I thank myself for spending countless hours diligently writing this book when fun in the sun was calling. My choice to spend time with the possibility of reaching you all, dear readers, is priceless.

The Deeper the Roots, the Stronger the Trunk, the Grander the Flowering.
—AMALIA CAMATEROS

Amalia Camateros

Amalia Camateros, award-winning poet and author, is a shamanic practitioner, empowerment guide, intuitive-energy healer and speaker who started her healing career in Australia as a naturopathic doctor and has worked in the field of health and consciousness for over thirty years. She was the private health practitioner for the famous Australian rock band INXS for over six years administering to their health during their grueling music tours in the early 90s.

She is an ordained minister, ceremonial priestess and workshop facilitator for breathwork, grounding and embodiment. She has also garnered a notable reputation as a powerful facilitator of her EarthSpirit Dance™ shamanic dance workshops and prayerformances at conferences, expos and events both nationally and internationally including for Alberto Villoldo, Jose Arguelles, David

Hawkins, Michael Beckwith, Robert Mirabal, Deepak Chopra, Neale Donald Walsch and David Wolfe.

As an Earth Spirit Wisdom guide, Amalia facilitates a healing journey for your personal needs either on the spiritual rocks of Sedona's vortexes or indoors for a more in-depth emotional core healing.

She is highly intuitive and skilled as an emotional tracker who shines the light on hidden shadows and locates the subconscious glitch and patterns of your psyche to bring them into conscious awareness for release and healing.

Amalia draws from a multi-modality base of healing experience and her own bank of wisdom and applies it to your personal needs. A strong emphasis is on helping you ground your mind and body with Mother Earth so that you can be a strong conduit of your highest potential and walk in the clarity of your spiritual embodiment. In all of her work she draws from and utilizes Earth's Wisdom to help you ground and anchor it as your own Body Wisdom.

Her first book, *Spirit of the Stones*, invites you on a remarkable real life shamanic journey "into" the sacred sanctuaries of the Earth, into a world where the rocks and mineral kingdom talk and reveal powerful wisdom for our higher purpose. Amalia crosses the borderlands of "reality" into the deeper recesses of Earth Wisdom with an ancient mission that relates with urgency a new revelation calling upon us to be true stewards of our planet. Real understanding of Nature's plan in the Ascension Process, and the Mineral Kingdom's role, is disclosed with vivid clarity. The time is NOW, the stones say!

Transmissions of Earth Spirit Wisdom: A Shamanic Way of Seeing, Being and Healing brings forth a distillation of intrinsic wisdom for a higher alignment of self. Although they are foundational, ancient teachings, this work is revealed once more after eons, bound in a modern compendium that will assist you in tapping into your own inner realms for emotional reconciliation and healing.

Visit
EarthSpiritWisdom.com

More Wisdom Teachings
with Amalia

OTHER BOOKS BY AMALIA

Read about Amalia's shamanic true life journey in her first book, *Spirit of the Stones: A Retrieval of Earth Wisdom*, to discover how to listen to Mother Earth's wisdom, tap into the Stone kingdom and embody your inner shaman.

COURSES

To learn more about how to ground and center your energy, Amalia has created a comprehensive but short online Shamanic Healing Course: "Stronger Than Ever—Shamanic Grounding Tools to Stabilize Your Energy." You can find that and more on Amalia's website at EarthSpiritWisdom.com under "Courses and Retreats."

CONNECT WITH AMALIA

To view Amalia's full list of healing services and to schedule a session or retreat with her, visit EarthSpiritWisdom.com.

WRITE TO AMALIA

amalia@earthspiritwisdom.com

STAY ON THE PULSE WITH AMALIA

Facebook.com/EarthSpiritWisdom
YouTube.com/AmaliaCamateros
Instagram.com/amaliashamama

I look forward to taking you deeper on your healing journey. Blessings,
—AMALIA